SHE SAID . . .
HE SAID . . .

SHE SAID . . .
HE SAID . . .

Teens Speak Out on Life and Faith

Edited by Laurie Delgatto
With Contributions by Janet Claussen and K. Sean Buvala

Saint Mary's Press   Winona, Minnesota

Genuine recycled paper with 10% post-consumer waste.
Printed with soy-based ink. 50413

The publishing team included Laurie Delgatto, development editor;
Gabrielle Koenig, copy editor; James H. Gurley, production editor
and typesetter; Cären Yang, art director and designer; Andy Palmer,
designer; manufacturing coordinated by the production services
department of Saint Mary's Press.

Cover art by Britta Feuerhelm, Winona, MN

Printed in the United States of America

Printing: 9 8 7 6 5 4 3 2 1

Year: 2011 10 09 08 07 06 05 04 03

ISBN 0-88489-742-7

Library of Congress Cataloging-in-Publication Data

She said— he said— : teens speak out on life and faith / edited by
Laurie Delgatto.
  p. cm.
Includes index.
  Summary: Writings drawn from submissions of almost 700
Catholic teenagers from throughout the United States, who
responded to the questions included in the book.
ISBN 0-88489-742-7 (pbk.)
  1. Teenagers—Religious life—Miscellanea. 2. Teenagers—
Conduct of life—Miscellanea. [1. Youths' writings. 2. Catholics.
3. Christian life.] I. Delgatto, Laurie.
BV4531.3 .S54 2003
248.8'3—dc21
                                                    2002010246

CONTENTS

A few years ago, back in the last century, a small group of women involved in various ministries with young people gathered to discuss the lives of adolescent girls. The principle that guided the discussion was the belief that human experience mediates spirituality. A plethora of literature about girls, based on research as well as anecdotal evidence, confirmed the age-old intuitive sense that girls' experience is unique to their gender.

The issue of gender differences was a driving force for this gathering, and the leaders clearly recognized that the world of adolescent boys had its own issues and challenges. If gender differences affect physical, emotional, and psychological development, then certainly spirituality is shaped as well by feminine or masculine perspectives. All young people must learn to navigate the waters of adolescence on their way to adulthood, but the challenges may be different for each gender. *She Said . . . He Said . . .* reveals both the similarities and differences of boys' and girls' responses to challenging questions about life and about faith.

Invitations to participate in the *She Said . . . He Said . . .* project went out to over five thousand schools and parishes across the country, inviting high school students to send us their responses to one (or more) of the questions at the end of each chapter. Almost seven hundred teenagers submitted their responses. The difficult process of deciding which ones to include in the book involved several readers from across the country evaluating each of the responses. The result is an insightful look into the world of adolescent thinking, worrying, dreaming, and soul searching.

The number of submissions Saint Mary's Press received from boys and girls was the most obvious gender difference: girls' entries accounted for almost 75 percent of the total received. This fact accounts for the greater number of girls' writings in this book. The number of responses to particular questions was also revealing. Friendship was by far the most popular topic with girls' musings, outnumbering boys' in this category five to one. Boys' favorite topics were spread out fairly evenly among friendship, fears, and values that they learned from their parents. Girls too had much to say about their parents.

The thoughts about family and parents were overwhelmingly positive from both genders. Questions that were specifically religious in nature—the meaning of the Eucharist, experiences of God, encounters with Jesus and other biblical and holy people—were less popular, though intensely meaningful.

With a book like this one, we are limited to a certain number of pages. All the responses we received are worthy of publication because they speak of the wisdom that young people have to offer one another and the world at large. We express gratitude to all the young people who took the time to write and share their thoughts.

So many youth ministers, religious educators, teachers, and parents continually support our efforts to make the voices of young people heard and known through books such as this one. We extend our deepest thanks to those who encouraged so many young people to put their words into writing and then sent them onto us.

And finally, I wish to thank Mary Koehler for all her administrative assistance with this project. I also extend my gratitude to Marilyn Kielbasa, Janet Claussen, and K. Sean Buvala, for the many contributions they made to this book and for their ongoing commitment to empowering young people, girls and boys alike.

This book is for young people by young people, but we hope that parents, teachers, counselors, and youth ministers will benefit from its wisdom as well. Enjoy this wonderful glimpse into the lives, hopes, and faith of young people.

Laurie Delgatto

Laurie Delgatto, editor

Teenagers Are Amazing

Teenagers are amazing.
I wish the world could see
Just how beautiful we are,
How compassionate we can be.

I wish they could take back
All the cynical things they've said
And see how much we shine,
Be positive instead.

Remark on our radiant smiles
And the differences we make,
All the people our lives touch,
All the changes we make.

I wish they could remember
How tough our lives can be.
The promises that are broken,
The violence in the streets.

Yet still we venture forward,
Unsure of where the road may lead,
Hoping they will notice
The changes that we've made,
The power we hold,
The wisdom we have hidden,
The stories yet untold.

I hope the world will notice
What some have already seen.
Teenagers are amazing people
Striving to follow their dreams.

—Yamilka I. Ventura, Bronx, NY

Two friends can sit on a porch swing for three hours **without saying a word** and walk away like it was the **best conversation** they have ever had.

—Janessa Ann Damico, Rochester, NY

Great friends **tell you** that **you have a chance** with your latest crush even when he's the lead singer in the most popular band in the United States.

—Erica Moore, Washington Township, NJ

ABOUT OUR FRIENDS

Friends are those people with whom we have **detailed conversations.** Even if they do not answer back, we know **they are listening.**

—Dan Kick, Athol Springs, NY

Acquaintances are easy to come by, but a **great friend** is hard to find.

—Sean Ryan, Briarwood, NY

If you speak, they listen.
If you call, they answer.
If you're down, they lift.
If you refuse, they coax.
If you're frustrated, they advise.
If you cry, they cry.
If you sulk, they cheer.
If you curse, they understand.
They finish your sentences
    And make a dream out of your nightmare.
They are the highest notes in your laughter
    And the brightest glow-in-the-dark stars on your ceiling.
They are number 1 on your speed dial
    And the reason your father blames you for the phone bill.
They are your opposite, your twin, and your partner-in-crime,
    While voluntarily becoming your emotional punching bag.
They are door openers, truth tellers, and mind readers,
    Main characters in your autobiography.

The song "Lean on Me," by Bill Withers, defines great friends. The song describes someone who is understanding and willing to make sacrifices, someone who wants to help his friend get through a tough time. This is what a perfect friend is. Such genuine care tends to become mutual. However, a person doesn't constantly go through tough times, which brings up the second part of a great friend. A great friend should also be capable of keeping good times rolling. He should try to keep his friend from getting down, and he should make their time together enjoyable. A great friend should also be willing to let his friends assist him when he is in need and they want to help. That completes the circle of mutuality, which is the basis of friendship.

—Name withheld, Middleton, CT

Why keep a diary
When they hold secrets safer than a locked book?
Best friends don't have to tell each other that they are
When actions speak louder than words.

—Norain Siddiqui, Morristown, NJ

I realized that a great friend is not just one who lends
a listening ear, offers a shoulder to cry on, or shares your secrets. Rather a
great friend is one who willingly accompanies you through life's various
moments, holding your hand through times of trial, sharing a smile
during days filled with laughter, and all the while encouraging you to
achieve your goals and aspirations. As years pass, a great friend is one
who undoubtedly remains by your side allowing you to grow separately
without growing apart. A great friend is a precious gift from God, deliv-
ered to aid you through life and assist you in becoming the person you
one day hope to be.

—Samantha Lynne Fusco, Worcester, MA

SHE SAID

A friend is someone you can trust.
A friend will never let you down.
He never leaves you when you're sad;
He cheers you up when you frown.
He's always there to listen,
Always willing to advise,
And if there is a fight,
He's always first to compromise.
Only one man is a lifelong friend.
His name is Jesus;
He is both human and divine.

—Tim Healy, Pontiac, MI

HE SAID

As I face increasingly difficult struggles in my life, I find myself drawing on the strength of my friends. I depend on them to listen to me and to understand, to tell me what I want to hear, and to talk me into doing what I need to do. I often wonder if I am a burden on them—too much of a drain on their energy. They never complain or say a word against me. They comfort me and drag me through the long days. We laugh together and have random adventures. I can't do anything without them. They are by no means perfect people. They have flaws and struggles of their own, but they care, and I could never ask for more.

—Jenny Torgerson, Claymont, DE

I see a friend as someone I trust and who is of value to me. A great friend, however, is that and more. A great friend knows everything about you. Your souls are so closely connected that you are practically bonded as one. You can tell a great friend from a regular friend. It's like finding your soul mate. You just know, and that's the greatest part. You'll know who your true friends are amongst all the people who may be

A great friend is hard to acquire and is far beyond any ordinary acquaintance. Once you find a great friend, you should always value this majestic gift. There are many factors and qualities in a great friend. Some people may think that a great friend is just a friend who treats them well. Other people look deep into the friendship when calling somebody a great friend, and I am one of those people. I thank God every day for my many friends, but there are a few distinguished, amazing people whom I would go far enough to call my great friends. They are my soul mates, my confidants, my brothers and sisters at heart.

I believe that great friends have a past together and that they each know what the other has endured over the years. Great friends are there when you celebrate the good times in your life. They are also there to help you through the bad parts. Great friends are those people who are happy to hear your voice after a long day at school. These outstanding people rush home to call you because they are eager to tell you that they made the honor roll or that they have been accepted to Harvard. No matter how envious they may be, great friends will be on the sidelines cheering you on during a victory.

—R. J. Y., Somerville, NJ

dishonest and untrustworthy. With all said, I thank God for the people I am blessed with. Every person I have met or will meet is important to me because they all affect my life in some way. To me a great friend is someone who has walked with me through the darkest times of my life and is still standing with me. To me a great friend is God.

—Michelle Apostol, Staten Island, NY

A great friend has the qualities of a hero.

Great friends don't come along just when you want them. True friends are one in a million. They have a personality that is always right for the occasion. They make you laugh when you think nothing can. They make you feel loved and wanted when you feel like you are worthless. They stand by you through everything. When you find a great friend, you wordlessly say that oath from the Book of Ruth, "Where you go, I will go; where you lodge, I will lodge. . . . and your God [will be] my God."

—Angela Riechert, Saint Louis, MO

What makes a good friend?

A good friend is someone who will listen to you.
A good friend will tell you the truth no matter what.
A good friend will catch you when you fall.
A good friend will stop other people from saying bad things about you.
A good friend will give you his last dollar if you need it.
A good friend will treat you like you want to be treated.
A good friend will put down what he is doing to help you.
A good friend will always make time for you.
A good friend is someone you can talk to about anything at any time.
A good friend is a shoulder to cry on.
A good friend is like a brother or a sister.
That is what makes a good friend.

—Brian D. Stephenson, San Diego, CA

Friends will come and go through the revolving door

on the threshold of my life. However, only a precious few will leave an imprint on my soul and stay with me until my dying day. Common threads are woven through all true friendships. One of these threads is trust. Without trust, the foundation on which a friendship is built would deteriorate, causing the whole relationship to collapse. You should be able to share your deepest thoughts, hopes, and fears with a true friend, no matter what. They share in your accomplishments and comfort you through tears. There is a sixth sense that exists between only the closest of friends. The best lessons learned cannot be read from a textbook; we must experience the joys and trials of this journey with our friends and look inside their souls to see life's truths. Great friends are extensions of ourselves, and they guide us through this obstacle course called life.

—Amber Brown, East Syracuse, NY

From womb to tomb,

From birth to earth,
Friends are always near.
They always guide you when you need help.
They always hold you dear.
They do not care where you are from,
But they do care where you are going.
They will quickly be at your side,
And they will not show signs of slowing.
They will always be there to hear your problems,
But friends will never judge you.
They will give you insight to steer you right,
And everything they say will be true.
Friends really care about how you feel;
They do not act fake, they always act real.
All these things you find in a friend,
A friend who is really sincere.

We find ourselves telling one another the deepest details of our lives—things we don't even share with our families. But what is a friend? a confidant? a shoulder to cry on? an ear to listen? a heart to feel? A friend is all these things and more. No matter where we met, no matter how long we have been together, I call you friend. It is a word so small yet so large in feeling, a word filled with emotion and overflowing with love. Once the package of friendship has been opened, it can never be closed. It is a book that is always waiting to be read and enjoyed. We have our disagreements and our disappointments, but we also have concern for one another. Friendship is a unique bond that lasts through all tribulations. Parts of us go into our friendships—our humor, our experiences, our tears. Friendships are foundations necessary for life and love.

—Lauren Bianchi, Dobbs Ferry, NY

These are the friends everyone should have,
For in them you have nothing to fear.

—Jason Mar-Tang, Staten Island, NY

A great friend is someone who is a positive influence in your life. They help you not only find mistakes in yourself, but they help you correct those mistakes as well. A great friend sticks by you during both the good times and the rough times in your life. They pick you up when you are down and help you to stay up when you are falling. They do not turn their backs on you, and they always remain faithful. A great friend is someone you can trust with secrets about your life that you would not want anyone to know. They keep you company when you need it. A great friend helps you do what is right in order for you to develop a greater relationship with God.

—Stephen Jacob, Cincinnati, OH

A great friend is a dream to most people. They believe that a great friend is like some fairy godmother who will smooth over all problems with a wave of her magic wand. They want a superfriend who is able to cure a blue day or a confrontation with someone faster than a speeding bullet. I have found no such friend, nor do I really wish to. You see, I don't believe that a great friend should be able to correct everything. I think that creates a relationship that mirrors a parent-child relationship rather than a friendship. A truly great friend is someone who goes through the same problems as everyone else and comes out of their trials a little better, or at least a little wiser. A great friend helps when they can, is honest about what they think, and will even put up with your complaining if the occasion calls for it. The hardest part of having a great friend is to remember that your friend needs a great friend too. It takes two people to make a great friendship. A great friend is like having your own private teddy bear that talks back to you to help you, guide you, or laugh with you.

—Olivia Paglia, Harper Woods, MI

A great friend is one who is completely open with you. A true friend will not purposely try to confuse you nor will he take advantage of you. He will not pretend to be your friend but really hate you. The real friend is on an equal level with you and is there to comfort and support you in your need. His interest in you is purely for friendship's sake and not to gain in any other way. When you are happy, he is happy. When you are sad, he is sad. There is nothing that he will not tell you, and he does not take satisfaction in your pain. A great friend is loyal to you.

—H. G., Rochester, MN

The definition of a great friend depends on the person who is creating the definition. To me a great friend must be someone you know will always be there for you. A great friend will hug you when you need it and help you up when you trip. A great friend is both truthful and loving. A great friend will dance with you even if you dance like your legs are having a seizure. The fact that they may be of a different gender, race, or faith shouldn't matter to them or to you. A great friend will tell you when your skirt makes your bottom look the size of the Titanic. A great friend will cheer you on even when you're losing and hug you like you won. A great friend should feel lucky to have you, and you should feel lucky to have them. A great friend is the kind you would have fun with at Wal-Mart. A true friend isn't afraid to say "I love you."

—Megan Howie, Danville, IL

If you want to be my friend, you need to have some desirable traits. The three that come to mind are honesty, fun-loving, and caring. I want a friend who will tell me the truth even if it's something I don't want to hear. I also want a friend who is fun to be with—if a person is easygoing with a sense of humor, he will be a great friend. A good friend needs to have a caring attitude. If I'm having a rough day, will he be there for me in my time of need? These are the three qualities I look for when I am deciding who my greatest friend will be. I must also display these same qualities so that I will be a great friend to someone else.

—Tim Ricker, Delphos, OH

SHE SAID

Only When . . .

Friendship is a rare jewel that shines
Only when you give it a sunny smile.
Friendship is a song that is sung
Only when you know its rhythms.
Friendship is a dream that comes true
Only when you believe in it.
Friendship is a sun that rises
Only when your heart has set on it.
Friendship is a throne on which you can sit
Only when you share your kingdom with it.
Friendship is a path that you will find
Only when you know you are lost.
Friendship is a hand that holds yours
Only when you extend yours.
Friendship is an album of memories you can leaf through
Only when you cherish it.

HE SAID

When we all look back to reflect on our lives, one of the questions that consistently emerges seems to pertain to our friends. We often ponder: Just who was the greatest friend in our life? We ask ourselves what makes a person a great friend. Some of the quick answers that come to mind are the qualities of loyalty, dependability, and honesty. I personally feel that none of these qualities are true indicators of friendship because anyone, even your greatest foe, can possess them. In my opinion, you have found a great friend when you know you would do anything and sacrifice everything in order to help that person, and they would do the very same for you. This is the single quality that is truly required in order to have a great friendship.

—Patrick Howard Jr., Athol Springs, NY

Friendship is a lantern that glows
Only when you need the warmth of it.
Friendship is a language you can speak
Only when you know the meaning of it.
Friendship is a potpourri of feelings you can smell
Only when you have a true friend.

—Cy Sison, Pontiac, MI

A good friend can be trusted to hear a secret. A great friend can be trusted to keep it. A good friend tells me jokes and makes me laugh. A great friend laughs at my jokes. Someone who will listens to your problems is a good friend. Someone who gives advice when it is needed is a great friend. Good friends, I believe, are those who know your most recent crush. Great friends will sit up with you during the night trying to think of ways to get him to notice you. Good friends don't care if you act like a dork. Great friends will join you in the act.

—Jaclyn, Omaha, NE

When I think of a great friend, I think of someone who is always there for me no matter what. They don't make fun of me for the things they know would hurt my feelings. They don't join in when other kids make fun of me. Instead, they stand up for me and tell the other kids to cut it out.

A great friend is someone who will help me get through things when I am having a hard time. A great friend is someone I can talk to when I feel the need to talk. They don't talk behind my back and never tell other people things I don't want them to tell. A great friend to me is someone who will stick by my side through the good and the bad.

—David A. Kotula, McSherrystown, PA

I have encountered many people in my lifetime. Some are mere acquaintances, some are companions when it suits them, and others cannot be trusted. Few have become great friends. A great friend is one I can count on to be there for me in all situations—in good times and in bad times, in joy and in sorrow. A great friend is a source of refuge, a person I go to when I am in need of comfort, wisdom, or strength. A great friend shows sincere loyalty and honesty without ever having to be tested. A great friend can bring out the best in me, even when I am at my worst. A great friend is one who expects the same from me, for a great friendship is shared by two people who are great friends to each other.

—Erin O'Connor, Morristown, NJ

20

Art by Troy Koehler, Winona, MN

My best friend left me—deserted me. Without a second thought, she just walked away. She knows what she wants, and I am standing in her way. Losing her has made me appreciate what a friend really is, or at least should be.

Friendship is a two-way street. Both people must respect each other as individuals and not take the relationship for granted. Even the best friendship could fall apart if it is neglected. Both friends must be honest, loyal, and supportive of each other through good times and bad times. A best friend is someone who can always be counted on, no matter what.

—Jacqueline Marie, Chelsea, IA

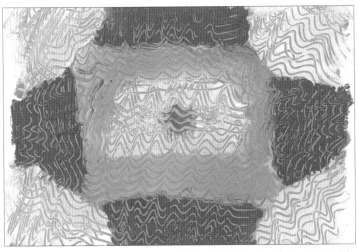

Art by Katie Appelwick, Winona, MN

HE SAID

Most of all, **they know** when you are feeling **loved** by the world, **hated** by the world, or just **lonely** in the world, and they **stand by your side** through it all.

—Katie Eileen Donovan, Saint Louis, MO

My friends are my **escape**. They are more **family to me** and are of more importance to me than **anything else** in the world.

—Lauren DelFavero, East Syracuse, NY

The main qualities of a noble friend are what the Holy Spirit bestows on us during the sacrament of Confirmation. The seven gifts are **courage** to do what is right, **reverence** to show profound respect to the Lord, **awe** for appreciating life, **wisdom** and **understanding** to proclaim the Good News, **right judgment,** and **fortitude** to endure pain and peril.

—Salvatore Mazzurco, Bronx, NY

A great friend is like a favorite movie that you watch over and over and **never get tired of.** Every time you watch it, you find out something different and new.

—Amanda, Maysville, KY

True friends are the people who ask you how you are and wait for an answer.

—Kristin Rossi, Pontiac, MI

A **part of you** belongs to them, and it is locked away like a **treasure** deep within their heart.

—Allison Marie Zimpfer, Buffalo, NY

Great friends **know what you're thinking** so well, they start taking the words right out of your mouth. . . . Great friends are like a **rare jewel;** they are hard to find and not easily forgotten.

—Selena Barnes, Brooklyn, NY

I think people use the term *best friend* too loosely. . . . There is a **gap between** having an **acquaintance** and having a **best friend,** and sometimes the gap is **blurred** in people's minds.

—Jeremiah McCarthy, Staten Island, NY

A great friend tells you when you are **wrong** and when you are **right,** not just when you are right.

—Thomas M. Bulow, Chicago, IL

What makes a good friend?

I ask, "Mom, how do you do what you do?"
And she tells me that **God is how** she does
what she does.

—Maureen Hayes, Magnolia, DE

Beauty is **skin deep** and can be changed,
but in the end **inner beauty** is not reversible.

—Karintha M. Ashe, Chicago, IL

ABOUT OUR
VALUES

My parents have always told me, "We will
trust you until you give us a reason not to."

—Matthew Dickman, Athol Springs, NY

A line of **communication** between parents
and children creates a strong relationship.

—Philip Muscarella, Hamburg, NY

Perhaps the most important lesson I have learned about being a parent is that parents never stop learning. I know that each child is different. They have different needs and wants, and they must be cared for equally but differently. It is imperative that each child's different emotions, feelings, and attitudes are taken into account. It is important that parents never claim to be anything more than humans who make mistakes and who are open to learning from their children. Children have so much to teach. Knowing when to be firm and when to be soft is also important. Personal feelings should never stand in the way of parents' being supportive and loving of their child. My goal as a parent will not be to have a cool or popular child; my goal will be to raise a loving, nurturing, and independent adult.

—Christina E. Laughter, San Diego, CA

I couldn't sleep. I had a guilty feeling inside me. The neat pack of cards I had won in the third-grade spelling contest today lay beside me. I wished I wouldn't have cheated. I didn't deserve the cards. I had to tell someone, so I woke my parents. They suggested I tell the teacher so that the prize could be given to the rightful winner. My parents have always taught me to be honest. Through their teaching me, I have developed a strong conscience that implants a terrible feeling in my stomach when I do wrong. Honesty is a value I hope I can keep with me for the rest of my life.

—Mark J. Mueller, Delphos, OH

"Don't worry about what other people think." I've heard that a million times from my mom. However, I didn't listen to my mother. We moved to a new town last year. When I started school there, I wanted everyone to like me. I tried my hardest to fit in. If everyone wore an orange shirt, I would do the same just to fit in.

One of my "friends" was the same way, and that was one of the reasons we got along. Then she started doing drugs to fit in. I wasn't going to stoop that low, so I told her she either had quit or stop hanging around me. She chose drugs. I got to thinking and realized I wasn't happy with my new self. I was busy trying to make everyone like me, but I didn't like me. The day I stopped worrying about what other people thought was the day I was truly happy. Like my mother says, "You shouldn't change for anyone."

—Jillian Cabrera, Hoboken, NJ

My older brother is married and has two children. Over the years I have observed how he and his wife have raised their two wonderful boys. I have noticed that my brother and sister-in-law always interact with their children in a positive fashion. Instead of constantly saying no to the child, they will divert his attention to something else, or they will politely remind him what he must do. There is no yelling or screaming, except for some crying here and there. The example of my brother and sister-in-law has shown me the value of having a positive attitude with children.

—Michael Nork, Middleton, CT

One of the great things that my parents have instilled in me is the value of free society and diversity. From the time I became able to formulate opinions and perform simple tasks, they allowed me to openly share my feelings, and they provided encouragement when my feelings and desires differed from theirs. I have been taught to respect all people, regardless of their race, creed, or culture. My parents demand respect from me, but they show me the same respect. My upbringing has made me realize that no one deserves to be discriminated against for any reason. All people are different, and it is this uniqueness that makes the world we live in so appealing. We are all children of God and should be treated as such. I am always encouraged to find out more about someone when I don't understand them instead of stereotyping them because of their differences and missing out on a potentially good friend. I firmly believe that if more parents would teach their children at young ages to take the time to understand and communicate with the people around them, our world would be much more peaceful, and people would be much more educated.

—Kenicia D. Adams, Harper Woods, MI

One of the values that I have learned from my parents is to never give up, whether it is related to my academic work, athletic programs, or my own personal goals in life. My parents have instilled this value in me and have taught me to believe in my abilities and in myself. Even if others may not believe in me, I must stay strong and keep my dreams and goals alive. This value has been extremely important to me in my academic work at school, in football and baseball, and in my own personal life. Even if a particular subject or a specific sports activity appears difficult at first, if you really have the desire and the heart to be the best you can be, you must persevere and maintain that drive to achieve your specific goals.

—Ryan Stearrett, Wilmington, DE

I have learned that if you are strict on a kid and show a lot of love, he will come up right. I learned that because my dad was always strict and didn't take anything from me, and now my brother and I are trying to do right.

—Durrell Johnson, Audubon, PA

My parents taught me that people with disabilities are a gift from God. They showed me this through their care of my brother, Danny.

When Danny was diagnosed with autism, my mom wanted to give him the best education possible. That required spending every day working with him on speech, occupation, and other skills. She had to enroll him in public school when he reached sixth grade because they had better services for him.

After Danny was enrolled, my mom realized that he was not getting all the services he needed. She started fighting the school board and after three years, the fight continues. She now homeschools Danny half-days.

My father takes Danny out on the farm and lets him help out, and never once has either of them complained. I believe God chose our parents for Danny because God knew that they would help the fight for rights of disabled people.

—Julie Huber, Perryville, MO

Having been born to two great parents, I feel that I have a good idea of how to be a good parent. My parents have been parenting for over twenty years now with my brother and me. They are certainly the people that have most shaped my life. It is in their fashion that I will one day raise my own children.

The biggest problems I see with parents today are over-parenting and under-parenting. Parents who meticulously watch over every single thing their child does will limit the child from learning from mistakes and also limit independence. Parents who let their children run wild all the time have children who lack proper self-control and can't acknowledge their improper actions. In addition to knowing how much to parent, laughter and sensibility, in my opinion, are the most important aspects of parenting.

—Ryan R. Thomas, Wilmington, DE

On June 8, 1984, a little girl was born into a world of love and comfort. That little girl was me. My mother was only eighteen at the time and did not know what she had in store for her. Her mother, my grandmother, asked her to leave the house because she wanted my mother to experience the world as it is since she decided to become a parent at such a young age.

My mother was faced with many hardships, but she overcame them all. As I got older, I saw my mother struggling just to make me happy, and I tried my best to help her as much as I could, mostly by doing chores like washing the dishes, sweeping the floors, dusting the furniture, and, of course, keeping my room clean. I always made sure I told my mom I loved her so that I could see her bright smile, and that smile always made my day brighter. My mother always made sure I was her first priority.

Now that I am seventeen, I know how much of a role model my mom is to me. She has taught me the love of family, and as each day passes, that love only grows stronger. As I continue with school and fulfill the rest of my life with my mom's guidance, I hope to be as strong and loving as

My parents have instilled in me the value of unconditional love. It is evident in their support when I attempt something new. My choices may not be theirs, but they respect my pursuit nonetheless. If I succeed, they rejoice. If I fail, they comfort. They do not say, "I told you so." Instead they encourage me to try again.

They are quick to forgive when I have done wrong. While they may be disappointed, their unconditional love allows me to admit my guilt and learn from my mistakes without having to fear that I will lose their love. This empowers me to follow my own conscience.

Unconditional love is seamless and everlasting. It does not depend on my grades, my clothes, or my choice of music. Unconditional love is what God gives his children and what my parents give me.

—Josh Fong, Ocala, FL

my mom was for me. I wish that on the day I become a mother, I will be able to create the same loving and comfortable environment I was born into on that fine June day.

—Amanda M. Kearns, Hoboken, NJ

A great value that I have learned from my parents is compassion for the sick and elderly. My parents took care of my great uncle who battled cancer for thirteen years. At times things got tough, but my parents never turned their back on him. Other family members were always too busy to help or even to visit, but we were always there when he needed us.

Often we had to give up our plans and holidays to spend many long hours in the emergency room when he was not well. I think I will always remember how grateful he was that we were there and that we cared so much for him. It gives me a good feeling to know that I am able to help someone, even if all I do is talk to them or keep them company.

—Stacie Tarris, Pottsville, PA

I have learned that your parents' relationship has a drastic effect on who you become and how you act. When I was six years old, my parents divorced. Ever since then I have viewed relationships as negative and hurtful. I began improving my outlook on relationships about two years ago. I had been with my girlfriend for almost a year, and I was in love. Then my father and my stepmother divorced, and a whirlwind of negative feelings sucked me back in. The relationship I was in ended, and all proceeding relationships have also faltered. Every time I get close to a girl, I break things off and run away. My personal scar has ruined many relationship possibilities. When I have children, my wife and I will be stellar examples of a loving couple. I will teach my children to have a positive, realistic view of love and relationships.

—Austin Zang, Baltimore, MD

I have learned from my parents the importance of family values. I have been taught to value honesty and obedience. I have been taught the importance of fulfilling my duties and being responsible in my studies and work. I have also been taught that it is important to love other people and to share what our family has with others. I have been taught to feel the presence of God and to trust in that presence.

—Saraih Sanchez, Nogales, AZ

One of the most important values my parents have taught me is the value of family. My family is the most important part of my life. My parents always tell me that no matter what happens, I will have a family who loves me and cares about me. No matter how hard it gets or how bad it is, my family will be there to help. My parents have shown me that family always comes first. Because of them I understand

There are many teachings that my parents have taught me, but there is one very important one that I will hold onto for the rest of my life. "Do not judge a book by its cover" is one of the most important principles for living that they have instilled in me.

This is very important to me because I am of a different ethnic background. I don't want to treat other people as I have been treated or judged. Acceptance of others is important to me, and I think every attempt should be made to rid myself of any type of prejudice.

This is good to learn because to judge anyone by their cover, their appearance alone, is dangerous. It is dangerous because we live in America, and America is so diverse. There are so many types of people in our country. Each one of them is unique with a different story and a different contribution to make.

—Timothy A. Nguyen, Dallas, TX

how important it is to have a strong and loving family. It is easy to get caught up in the world around us, and sometimes people can forget about what really matters. Nothing is worth losing your family. I will always remember the security I feel in my family, and I hope that someday I will have a family of my own that will be just as strong.

—Colleen Ferguson, Worcester, MA

The greatest value that I have learned from my parents that I will hold onto for the rest of my life is honesty. Honesty starts with being honest with yourself. My parents taught me that honesty starts with the small things in life and then the big things just take care of themselves. Honest people are respected and trusted. Be honest with others. Start with yourself.

—Sarah Lavelle, San Diego, CA

My mother has taught me an invaluable lesson in altruism: service is the rent you pay for room on this earth. On one freezing February morning when I was a first grader in China, I had to arrive at school punctually, despite the foot of snow and ice on the unplowed streets. This is not an easy feat when the normal mode of transportation is a bicycle, and there are no school buses or snow cancellations. Not wanting me to trek through the blanket of snow, facing dagger-like wind and blizzard-like conditions, my mother obtained some cardboard and rope from our neighbors and built a makeshift sled for me. Wrapped in layers of warm clothing, I enjoyed the sled ride as my mother arduously pulled me for a mile to school. My mother's act of self-sacrifice inspired me to follow her example.

—Stephen Meng, Middleton, CT

Dear God,

Thank you for giving me such a wonderful blessing. Without it, I don't know what I would do. This blessing has taught me many great things, and the values I learned from my blessing will stay with me forever. But the most important thing I was taught was to treat others the way I would like to be treated. Without that value, I would not have learned everything I've learned today. Whenever I am nice to others, they usually treat me the same, and I always learn something new from them. Another thing my blessing has taught me is that if I work hard to achieve my goals I can do anything. Without this lesson, I would be lazy and would not work to my potential. So thank you, God, for blessing me with such wonderful parents.

Love,
Kristeen

—Kristeen, Rockaway Park, NY

I have learned that a parent must be strong yet flexible. The parent is in charge of the household, not the child. The parent assigns responsibility and makes sure the tasks at hand are completed. And when something does not go as planned, the parent must take action accordingly. If punishment is needed, an appropriate punishment must be given. If something occurs beyond the child's control, the parent needs to deal with it in the best manner possible. The parent must be open to change.

Parental responsibilities include the education of the child. The parent should provide a visible example of appropriate behavior.

—Donald Aubrecht, East Aurora, NY

Art by Lisa Bork, Winona, MN

I have learned that being a parent is a big responsibility. God has a special plan for every child. As a parent, it will be my
job to provide my children with the education and the tools to help them
grow and follow God's plan. I will remember that children learn from
their mistakes and that they learn by their parents' example. I will show
my children how important it is to be honest and to trust each other.
When they do something wrong, I won't be mad at them. I will be
disappointed in them. I will show them that I believe in them, and they
will work hard because they won't want to let me down.

—Erik, Worcester, MA

HE SAID

One of the most important things that I know will come in handy is listening. . . . Just because **parents are older** does not mean they can't **learn** from someone younger than them.

—Jonah Sprehe-Costello, Saint Louis, MO

No matter how busy we were, we always sat down to a **family dinner.** Five familiar faces crowded around the table, not only to eat, but also to talk, laugh, fight, and as the years went by, grow.

—R. Facchini, Jersey City, NJ

My parents always **remind me** that every time I make a decision I am **becoming** the person I will be in forty years.

—Tony Huth, Cincinnati, OH

The most important thing my parents ever taught me is that the only thing in life you can **count on** is **change**. . . . The knowledge that my family will always be there for me no matter how I change is the greatest lesson I have ever learned.

—Lynn Orlandella, East Syracuse, NY

While I am not free of prejudicial feelings, I work hard to **accept people** for what they are. I try not to formulate opinions of people before I know them **regardless of their appearance or reputation.**

—Jess Cebulka, Somerville, NJ

My parents **never yell** back at me, even when I deserve it. They teach me to fight fire with water, not fire.

—Elizabeth M. Akerley, Tyngsboro, MA

One of the best things you can do for kids is **listen to them**. . . . I know that when I am a parent, I will ask my kids what they think, I will listen to them, and I will **love them**.

—J. A. M., Magnolia, DE

One of the greatest values I've learned from my parents is simply to love. . . . I believe that love is the **life-giving food**, nourishing us with the mysteries and joys of life. Without it, we **cannot survive**.

—Michelle Straub, Saint Louis, MO

From my parents I have learned that it is the **time you share** with your children, not the money you give them, that makes you a good parent.

—Kristen Sanchez, Washington Township, NJ

The main moral lesson my mother taught me was that whatever you put **into the world** comes back to you.

—Tawhanna Wood, West Islip, NY

The great value I have learned from my parents is the ability to **see beyond myself.**

—Elizabeth Troisi, Oyster Bay, NY

The most important value that my parents taught me is to **go to God** in prayer.

—Ijeoma Oguagha, Brooklyn, NY

Although my family is Catholic, my parents started celebrating the Jewish holiday of **Hanukkah** to teach my older sisters and me the importance of learning about and **tolerating other cultures and religions.**

—Danielle Turner, New Bern, NC

My parents have **always trusted** each other. This has given them the **freedom** to live their own lives without constantly worrying about the other person feeling insecure in the relationship.

—Walter Hafner, Aumsville, OR

MY THOUGHTS

What great value have you learned from your parents
that you will hold onto for the rest of your life?

39

Art by Emily McGann, Winona, MN

My greatest fear as I get older is that I will be the **exact same person** I am right now, that I will **never become** the person I am capable of being.

—Brianne Callahan, Aurora, IL

I fear failure in life. Even as I sit here, I know the girls that are sitting around me are **spinning out amazing essays** that will probably put mine to shame.

—Meghan Doherty, Newton, MA

ABOUT OUR FEARS

I don't want to **look back** five, ten, or even fifty years from now and say I that have made **too many mistakes.**

—Andrew Drejewski, Danville, IL

As I grow older, my greatest fear is not meeting **God's expectations.**

—Timothy J. Newlin Jr., Peoria, IL

In grammar school, there were always kids in the sandbox who would let me play make-believe princesses with them. In middle school, I wore the walking shorts with tights and loved Leonardo DiCaprio, and I was accepted into the group. Now in high school, I don't obsess (publicly at least) about my grades. I love being crazy. I make people laugh, and that's how I make my friends. Yet as I look to the future, at college and beyond, I am most fearful of being alone.

I have known my socially labeled "clique" since sixth or seventh grade. We've bonded over dumb jokes and a love of disco. But when I go to college, is anyone going to find me funny, or am I funny only in high school? I sit here and wonder how I am going to learn to make friends in the real world.

—Lydia Marston Albanesius, Morristown, NJ

My greatest fear when I grow up
is that life for me will be very rough.
I might run from my problems
because they are too tough.
I might not wash the dishes in the sink,
I might live my life drink after drink.
One of my greatest fears is
that I might be a bad father to my kids
or I might grow up to be a lazy slob,
and I won't be able to keep a job.
My greatest fear by far
is that I might drive reckless in my car.
But wait, my greatest fear is not not having a job,
but it's that I might lose the relationship I have with God.

—Garland Dane Morris, Brooklyn, NY

I may only be fourteen years old, but my thoughts on my greatest fears have deeply changed throughout my short little life. You see, when I was younger, I was always afraid of heights and very loud noises. Let's put it this way, I was afraid of almost everything. I guess you could have called me a scaredy cat. I was afraid of being put into a new environment with different people, I was afraid of rides, I was afraid of death, I was afraid to try new foods that didn't look very appealing, and so on. My view of my fears has changed greatly since September 11, 2001. Now everything I feared as a child seems so minuscule. I am now afraid of war, of living a life without peace, of having our freedom taken away, and of being struck again by terrorism. I pray for peace and love!

—Francesca Landolina, Staten Island, NY

43

Failure. As I've grown over the years, this particular fear seems to trouble me like a giant splinter. "Intellectually gifted" is how I've been labeled over the years. This label has been both a blessing and a burden in my life. Being smart can open up many doors in one's life, some leading to success and wealth. However, being smart also adds plenty of unwanted stress and pressure to one's life. This stress and pressure has been the origin of my greatest fear: failure. It scares me to think of what my life would be like if I weren't smart; I wouldn't have the bright future I have ahead of me now. My fear of failure has been more than just a hindrance to me; it has pushed me to want to overcome my fear and succeed in life, utilizing the opportunities I've been blessed with.

—Clay Odenweller, Delphos, OH

I am almost sixteen years old, and my peers have not yet pressured me. Since the fourth grade, when I first realized that evil exists in the world, I've always told myself that if someone offered me drugs or alcohol, I would turn them down. No problem. Nobody could push me into doing something that I didn't agree with. But lately I discovered differently. I learned that I don't have the self-confidence I need to go against the crowd. I don't want to mess up my life with premarital sex or smoking, but I am afraid that I'll meet the one guy or the best friend whom I can't say no to. When I first realized this, it scared me. I am worried that the moment I am put into an uncomfortable position, I won't have the courage to stick by my convictions and just say no.

—Sarah M. Robinson, West Chester, OH

I remember one day in one of my classes a bunch of the kids were talking about phobias. One kid said he was afraid of everything, and we all found that pretty amusing. I remember this because all I could think was that I wasn't afraid of anything. But I am.

44

My greatest fear, which becomes clearer as I get older, is the fear of being alone. I fear not having anyone to laugh with, to have fun with, or to hug when I feel down. What if something happens to me, and no one wants to be near me anymore? What if there comes a time when no one loves me, and I am always alone? I know that I never have to worry about this fear because someone will always love me. That some-one is God. I can talk to him, and he will always be there for me. My fear is the most powerful when I sin. It moves me further away from God and closer to being alone.

—Jonathan Harvey, Lawrence, MA

As I get older, I get to know myself. But what if I never find out who I really am? Even worse, will I like me?

So far I know only little bits about myself, but they're only things that everyone is, like being smart, being nice, and other stuff. But what makes me stand out? All my friends have endless qualities that make them special, and I want to know what my special quality is.

—Stephanie Sobon, East Syracuse, NY

My greatest fear as I get older is that I will forget. That I will forget past experiences and memories. That I will forget how to play and how to have fun. That I will forget about the wonderful friends that I have now. That I will forget how to rest and take time for family. That I will forget to stop every once in a while to focus on the world's beauty. That I will forget the lessons I've learned from my parents. That I will someday forget my morals and values. That I will forget how to be happy. That I will forget how to see the good in others. And most of all, that I will forget God.

—Kathryn Allen, Saint Joseph, MI

45

I have this image of a modern workplace where hundreds of men and women, each wearing the same tie or blouse, sit in hundreds of ergonomically designed chairs, in front of hundreds of computer screens, in a farm of cubicles. Each worker wears a can-do smile and has a yes-sir attitude in order to climb his or her way up the corporate ladder. My greatest dread is to become a member of this microsociety and to work merely for monetary reward. I feel that humans have the power of knowledge for a reason. This gift should be used to investigate the workings of the universe, or to solve the problem of hunger, or to write a great novel. I sincerely hope that as I grow older I can avoid this fear and avoid squandering my mind.

—John Rutherford, Cincinnati, OH

Throughout life we experience many fears. Some are little and some are more serious. Growing older brings many fears into young people's lives, especially my own.

My greatest fear as I grow older is that I will fail. Being a junior in high school, I have no idea what I want to become, and that scares me. I want to be very successful and get a good education. My fear is that if I fail, I will not be able to teach my children what I know. I want people to respect me for who I am. I want to be a leader and not a follower. As I grow older, I search for answers to my future and signs that may push my interests toward something that I can be successful in.

As I grow, I realize that time and patience are important virtues in my road to success.

—Jennifer Capowski, Dobbs Ferry, NY

My greatest fear as I get older is failing. Failing anything, great or small, is my worst fear. For example, failing to do well on the sports field could mean failing the team. They would all come down on me, and their success would not be any thanks to me. Failing to do well in the classroom scares me because that is failing my future. What I do not do well today will reflect on my job, my family life, and my future as a whole. Failing my parents means I have disappointed them in some way. This also means losing their respect, trust, and even their love. I do not know if I could handle that. So my goal in life is to succeed in everything I do. I know that God has this plan for everyone, but it will take some work on my part. I need to work to succeed. We cannot rely solely on God to solve our problems. Although God helps us greatly, we have to have a hand in it too.

—Chris Norman, Stayton, OR

As I have grown up, I have learned about the real world and its positives and negatives. I have learned what can cause happiness and what can cause heartache. My greatest fear, which can cause me great agony, is getting raped. I am petrified of going to a college because I could be attacked and then be in emotional pain and misery. In my mind, getting raped can cause great distress and serious emotional depression. This is a great fear to me because I know a girl who was raped while she was at college and had to be hospitalized because she was severely depressed. Rape is something that causes an emotional pain that can never be taken away or replaced.

—Joanne H. Gallahue, Newton, MA

My greatest fear lies in the troubling times
we are now experiencing and the future they promise. If the world ever gave me a sense of security, it no longer does. With so much evil clearly visible in the news and media, I wonder what world my future wife and children will live in. As I leave high school, go into college, and begin working, my world will undoubtedly change—for better or worse—leaving me to continually question my future and that of the world. Everybody talks about the light at the end of the tunnel, the goal that once achieved will grant happiness to all. But all I see is a planet full of people radically divided on anything and everything, from race to politics to religion, speeding through space without a care in the world. And I am scared.

—David S. Zubricki, Palos Park, IL

My greatest fear as I get older

is being forced to see what
my eyes have become tired of.
I fear that I won't
be able to walk the streets and simply
enjoy my feet hitting the concrete.
I fear that my opinions will go
unheard because I am the minority.
I fear that the majority will
still deny the right of equality.
I fear that wars will never
end their bloodshed.
I fear that unfortunate
people will still be crowding the streets,
trying to sleep.
I fear that we will continue ignoring those
unfortunate souls sleeping instead of waking
them up to take them home with us.

My greatest fear as I grow older is that I will forget what it is
like to be young. I have always heard my parents saying things that make
growing older seem like developing into a different person, things like,
"I'm too old for this," or "I can't take this anymore." When I grow older,
I want to be able to do the things I love doing now—sports, going out all
night, and just hanging out and having a good time—without worrying if
my body can take it or not. I want to be able to live for the moment and
have the moment be great, not painful or stressful because I am old.
When I do grow too old for the things I do now, I hope I will remember
how it was when I could do those things, so at least in my mind I will be
young forever.

—Kevin, Dallas, TX

I fear that my children will see what I have been forced to see,
the fear that only one person can be blamed—me!

—Vanessa C. Mahoney, Brockton, MA

My greatest fear as I age is complication. I fear that I will
be unable to find beauty in falling leaves, excitement in the first snow
cone of summer, or joy in taking a long, jacketed walk in almost-too-cold
weather. I fear that I will become bogged down with life—the worry, the
money, and the reality—to the point where simplicity will fail to exist. I
am afraid that in this loss of simplicity I will be at a loss with God. I most
fully see God in simple pleasures, the seemingly inconsequential joys that
make my life fruitful. God speaks to me in falling leaves and jacket
weather. If I lose sight of these things, then I invariably begin to lose sight
of God. I pray for perspective and clarity, now and as I grow older.

—Catherine St. Clair, Little Rock, AR

My greatest fear is being drafted to war. It would
be so terrifying to see what happens out there, to know that you could be
killed any second, or to have to kill someone else. The worst thing about
being drafted would be being away from my family and leaving them to
wonder if I will come back alive. Being severely injured would be an awful
thing too. Knowing that I cannot play sports and possibly hurting my
kids' reputations because they have a handicapped father is my greatest
fear, and I hope it never will happen.

—Justin Lulay, Aumsville, OR

My greatest fear as I get older is that my children will not have the same opportunities that I have. The world seems to be changing so fast, and the world we live in now is not the same as our parents' world. I fear that so much will have changed that things like the environment and family will not matter anymore. Everything is being done electronically now, and as time goes on more and more will be done this way. As we rely more on technology, our world will become smaller, and we will be talking to our family members on visual phones and seeing nature through computers. The world will become very impersonal and cold. I fear we will lose touch with humanity and nature. When we lose touch with these things, we will be giving up and wasting the beauty of the world God created for us.

—A. K., Demarest, NJ

My greatest fear as I get older is that I will become a product of the world around me. My mother taught me right from wrong when I was a child. She also taught me to try my best and to strive to be successful. While these are good lessons, I found that in order to be successful, one usually has to cheat or step on someone else's back to get ahead in life.

This is what goes on every day all over the world. I don't want to be the type of person to do those kinds of things. As I grow up, I've become used to clichés like "Nice guys finish last." This seems to be the case in the world around me.

I fear that one day I will have to conform to my environment because it may be a matter of my survival. Thus, success may turn me into a monster.

—Jamaal Patterson, Brooklyn, NY

Twelve years from now, I can just picture it: a huge "Welcome Back Class of '04" banner, a small table with name tags ready to be handed out, and hordes of people milling around sipping punch from clear glasses and talking animatedly with old friends. My greatest fear is my ten-year high school reunion.

What will I have done by that time? Will I be a success or a failure? Will my classmates look at me and think: "She was so smart. I wonder where she went wrong?" Or will they say, "I always knew she would make it." Maybe I will be a success in terms of career, family, and money, but what will I be thinking, sitting there drinking my punch? Will those things be important any longer? Maybe my more important accomplishments will be pulling a friend out of a jam, offering a smile on a rainy day, or picking someone up who's been pushed down. But will my peers recognize that kind of success? Will they see past material things to find that I have accomplished a lot more on a deeper level? Of course, that should be their greatest fear, not mine.

—Allison Elwer, Delphos, OH

51

My greatest fear, and probably my only fear, is that I will not be a good father or husband. Actually it is quite terrifying to me. I want to be there for my family when they need me. I have to remember that running away from a situation will not solve problems. I don't know what I would do if I was a father who left my wife and kids. I wouldn't even deserve the title of father. I don't want my kids to grow up without me. I don't even want to use death as an excuse.

—Jason F. King, Brooklyn, NY

My greatest fear as I get older is not death or loneliness. I am not frightened of physical suffering or mental deterioration. Rather, I am afraid that I will go through what every other generation has gone through, is going through, or will go through. I am afraid that future invincible youth, like me right now, will fail to see the dignity in my years.

I have often found myself disrespecting and being blind to the gifts and talents of those who came before me. I am guilty of a lack of understanding and of affecting a nonchalant superiority and an apathetic attitude toward those who offer me wisdom and compassion. I have succumbed to the isms of society, and I wonder if my sins will come back to haunt me.

52

As age sweeps me off my feet like a high-speed train, I don't anticipate the future; I fear the future. In a lifelong journey attempting to find an inner light to my faith, I realize that Catholic morals no longer stand up in society. This being my trepidation for the future, it appears that Catholic morals are decaying like human bones that are exposed to carbonization. This comes from having witnessed many friends and family members disregard Catholic teachings on sex, abortion, and the Scriptures. In fact, some friends have gone so far as to renounce their belief in Jesus, feeling inclined to take on a deist attitude.

What I fear for the future is that Catholics, as well as Christians universally, will become a disrespected sect. In fact, what I fear in the future is a resurgence of Christian persecution. Has our faith become so discomforting that it's okay to reject Jesus and disregard his rules? My fear is one concerning the outlook for Catholics.

—Ryan Prentice, Chicago, IL

Like an empire withering into oblivion, so too must I reach my golden age and fade. Maybe like the Greeks' and Romans', my glory will be remembered. Is it possible to hope?

Perhaps my flesh and blood will notice my body's demise, and I will become ugly to them. Instead of being nurtured with tenderness in my last few days, I could be put away in a nursing home, or worse, be neglected, exploited, and abused.

No communication. No escape. No love.

My greatest fear as I get older is to die unappreciated by the people I love the most.

—Kristine N. Nadal, San Diego, CA

My greatest fear as I get older is dying from someone else's carelessness. People today are not careful. For instance, people accidentally shoot each other when they are playing around with guns, or hurt each other when they are playing around in general, just trying to be funny. And to be honest, I am scared to die. Every time I think about it, I get down, even though I know I'm going to heaven.

—William C., Audubon, PA

As I get older, many of my childhood fears are gone. I am no longer afraid of the monster in my closet or what is lurking in the dark. My fears have progressed, not gone away. They now consist of anthrax scares, terrorist attacks, and being alone.

My greatest fear, however, is that I am wasting my life. I try to make every day, every minute count. After the recent tragedies of September 11, 2001, I have learned how short life is. It seems almost stupid to be doing homework when I could be taking a walk or simply enjoying the holiday season. But I know that education is a very important part of life and that in the future I won't regret it.

I try not to be sad, or wallow in self-pity because that is a definite waste of time. Every single day is a gift from God, and I am determined not to waste any of them. This may seem like a daunting task for a fourteen-year-old, and I don't doubt that it is. My greatest fear is that in seventy years my life will be all regrets, and I will do anything I can to stop that from happening.

—Molly McDonald, Worcester, MA

Art by Peter Singer-Towns, Winona, MN

I'm honestly **afraid** of the word *college.*

—Nicole Prater, Saint Louis, MO

My greatest fear is not of getting older, rather it is of **growing up**. I fear losing that part of me that always **wants to have fun.**

—Jenna Dykstra, Los Angeles, CA

Nuclear weapons, war, prejudice, and impertinence have instilled great fear in me. My greatest fear is that we, as a maturing society, will not be able to deter such evils. I am afraid that we will not be able to maintain a **reasonable balance** between the **good and evil** that is necessary for continual growth.

—Name withheld, Staten Island, NY

I'm scared of the fact that as I grow older and move on to bigger and better things I might **forget where my roots** are. I might get caught up in my work and forget my family and friends, **who have made me** the person I am today.

—Kevin Lao, Detroit, MI

I fear most the time I am **called to die.** I am afraid of growing up, getting married, having kids, and then having **something tragic happen to me,** and I leave my kids without a mother.

—Becca Gasiewicz, Grove City, PA

The path that I will follow in life is going to be **forever twisting and turning** in different directions, and I will always be unaware of what could be around the corner. The **scariest thing** in life is not knowing.

—Alexis Starr Gentile, Hoboken, NJ

My greatest fear as I get older is that I may **forget how to dream.**

—Rika Nakano, Seattle, WA

My biggest fear is **losing the innocence** I possessed as a little girl.

—K. A., Tyngsboro, MA

I want to **prove my dad wrong** because I know he thinks it's a matter of time before I screw up. **Being a failure** might not scare others, but it sure scares me.

—Camilla Elizabeth Coffin, Seattle, WA

Ever since I was a young boy, it's always been my goal that when I leave the world, I leave behind **as a legacy memories** of what I did. The worst thing to happen in my eyes is to not be remembered. If **no one remembers** your life, it would seem like you had never even existed.

—C. G., Middleton, CT

My greatest fear is that I will continue to lose **my curiosity and my drive** to seek answers about the **meaning of life.**

—Gina Nicole Stabile, Dobbs Ferry, NY

When you're little, you **can't wait to get older,** to grow up and have a car. But when you're grown up, you **wish you were a kid again** because of the things you could do as a kid but can't do anymore.

—Nick Ryan, West Islip, NY

My greatest fear as I get older is that it will become increasingly difficult to find Christians around me who **live their lives** in a way that I can look up to.

—Brendan Kalish, Oxnard, CA

Am I going to **make myself happy?** This may seem like a no-brainer to accomplish, but it seems to me I **do certain things** to make other people happy and forget about my own wishes.

—Laura Ashley Larson, Fullerton, CA

MY THOUGHTS

What is your greatest fear as you get older?

One thing that makes me happy is prayer. **No amount of money, cars, or clothes** can ever replace the happiness of prayer, which has had such a wonderful effect on my life.

—Name withheld, Canton, OH

Happiness is **a night without homework.**

—Katie Bradley, Omaha, NE

ABOUT OUR JOYS

Some things that **make me happy** are skateboarding, snowboarding, and riding my dirt bike or my Jet Ski.

—Joe, Riverhead, NY

I love seeing people happy because of me. I want to **live my life** to the fullest by helping others enjoy life to the fullest.

—Andy Lanigan, Athol Springs, NY

Something that makes me happy is seeing teen-agers of different races holding hands, being friends, and just getting along. Too many people in our world today are still living in the past and think everyone should stay with their own race and not communicate with anyone else who is even remotely different from them. Yes, we do have schools with blacks and whites in them, and yes, we do see a lot of people from those two races hanging out together, but what about the Native Americans, the Vietnamese, and the Chinese? When I see those select few who don't let color get in the way of their relationships, it makes me happy. Going to the mall and seeing a white girl and a black boy holding hands is just absolutely beautiful to me. It brightens my heart and lifts my spirits.

—Audery Bakke, Saint Louis, MO

There are several things in life that can make every-one happy. Some of these things are wealth, clothes, and other material possessions. Those things can occasionally turn into false gods. On the other hand, there are other people who don't need to buy anything

Singing loudly, double chocolate chip ice cream, playing guitar, rolling down hills with friends at night, stars, the ringing in the ears that one falls asleep with after a rock show, playing in the rain, road trips, beaches, campfires and s'mores, hot chocolate in the summer, hot chocolate in the winter, running, surprising someone with a present, smiling, sleeping in on Saturdays, writing, reading good poetry, hearing friend's poetry, long car rides, finishing great books, swimming at two in the morning, friends who call themselves Megatron, jean jackets, Keebler Soft Batch cookies, tree houses, nostalgia, corduroy, break dancing, tickling, talking with friends until sleep comes, talking with friends instead of sleeping, surprise endings, yelling oneself hoarse at a high school football game, fighting the good fight, doing something without being asked, Wiffle ball, Christmas, backyard football, pumpkin pie, getting dirty while working hard, singing loudly with friends, and hugs.

—Jeremy Mosher, Cincinnati, OH

material to make them joyful. As one of these people, I know that I can be glad with everything God-given and nothing man-made.

The things that make me happy are the simple things in life. I never need money or anything man-made to make me content. One of the things that makes me content is just being with my family and friends. What I like most about being with my friends and family is the fact that I can easily make them laugh. It constantly makes me happy when I see others laughing.

Many other things make me blissful. I'm blissful when it's raining and when the sun is shining brightly. Everything about nature makes me happy. In fact, everything natural can make me happy, such as my God-given talents, my family and friends, and being a beautiful person on the inside. In conclusion, my life is full of joy, which makes me joyful and glad to be alive.

—Rajinder Mahil, Jamaica Estates, NY

I am happy when I have something to talk about with my dad. When I was younger, my dad and I used to talk to each other all the time. However, now that I am older, I don't have as much free time with my dad as I used to. We just say "good morning" when we wake up and "good night" when we go to bed. The rest of the time, there is little communication between us.

However, when we talk about different things, whether it's cars, computers, or anything at all, I feel happy inside. It is a special feeling that makes me feel like I'm on top of the world. It makes me feel a lot closer to my dad, and I would like to have that feeling more often. I also know he feels better too, and that's what makes me feel happy.

—Afshawn Towfighi, Fort Lauderdale, FL

What makes me happy is being with my friends. We have fun together and we get along great. We enjoy one another's company and have a lot of laughs together. Also just the sense of being together gets me into a happy mood.

What also makes me happy is when I draw. It is one of my favorite hobbies. Drawing relaxes me and gives me peace of mind. Besides, I love drawing, and I am great at it. I could draw for hours and would never get sick of it.

Helping people out also makes me happy. I feel that I did something good for someone. I also feel that I helped someone out in a small but very good way.

I just became a Eucharistic minister. Giving out the host at Communion makes me feel like I am Jesus in the world today. I am giving out the body of Christ to others. These are just a few of the things that make me feel good. But there are many other things that make me feel happy.

—Lindsey Staber, West Islip, NY

Some of the things that make me happy are fishing, playing basketball, hanging out with my friends, and especially being with my parents. Also, the most important thing that makes me happy is being able to know, serve, and love my creator, Jesus Christ!

I am happy when I am fishing because I am with my dad and brother, alone in the nature having fun. I catch the cool little fish and then release them right back to where they came from.

Second, I am happy when I am playing basketball because God gave me the talent to play. I also like basketball because my dad was my coach almost every year, and together we both accomplished many goals.

I am happy when I am with all my friends because I know I can depend on them no matter what I ask them. They help me when I'm feeling sad, take care of me when I need it, and we all have fun in each other's company.

As I sit on a boardwalk bench or walk down a busy downtown sidewalk, I see so many different people. Bookworms and jocks, punks and preps, boys and girls, blondes and brunettes, enabled and lame, each has his or her own unique post, current struggles and joys, and promising future. I love people. A chance to glean insight into another's world lingers in every conversation. Why throw that away? It is up to me to grasp that opportunity.

Some see challenge and adventure in travel or daredevil stunts. My adventure is finding common ground. What if I didn't take that chance, ignored a girl because she was darker skinned or a boy because he had a Mohawk? I may miss the chance of a lifetime, the chance to make a friend. People make me happy.

—Liz Scanlon, San Diego, CA

I am happy knowing Jesus in this life because I know I will live forever with him in the next part of my life.

These are a few things that make me happy in my life, and I never want to lose any one of these things.

—Stephen A. Liberty, South Amboy, NJ

The thing that makes me happy the most is my family. I have a very big family, and I love being with them. Sometimes we fight, and sometimes we get mad at one another. But we are strong enough to overcome our fights, forget about them, and move on. We are very lucky to have this because many people do not have a big family to be surrounded by. That is why I love being with my family and doing things with them. I love spending time with them, and I wouldn't have it any other way. My family is my happiness.

—Joseph M. Mitchell, Chicago, IL

It has always seemed that happiness is hard to achieve, that it takes a lot of something really special to be happy. However, I have found that it is the little and supposedly unimportant things that make me happiest. For many people, happiness is the nonchalant conversations and jokes made at the lunch table. Even a glance from a crush is really important. Complimenting someone's new shoes or remembering to make a birthday card will initiate happiness in other people. Money is not needed for happiness, but sometimes it's hard to remember what is.

—Name withheld, Bronxville, NY

I am happy when enjoying life's simple pleasures, such as watching the sunset or falling asleep on the beach to the sounds of ocean waves. Such unpretentious things make me happy because I feel in tune with nature, the work of God's hand. I am happy when I run solo because the deep solitude allows me to separate my mind from the concerns of the rest of the world. But I am surely most happy when I can feel the presence of God in my life.

—Rachel Morrison, Tyngsboro, MA

The wind whistles past my ears and the sun blinds my eyes as I ride my bicycle through my world. My legs pump with passion and fury, ever increasing the distance between my starting mark and me. No element of nature can slow my will to ride. The heat, snow, and rain can never steal the happiness I gain when riding my bike.

The thrill of dodging traffic, negotiating tight turns, and making repairs with duct tape surges deep into my heart. Whether I am skidding down a road or sliding face-first down a dirt path, I offer a heavenly smile, filled with joy. The speed of living brings happiness and tranquility to my mind.

—Patrick Ross III, Hamden, CT

There are really a zillion things that make me happy. If I had to pick one thing, it would be teaching religious education at my church. I swear it's one of my favorite things to do. At first I thought I wouldn't like it. I mean, it was volunteer work so it simply seemed like a hassle. But I was hooked after the first class. There is no better feeling in the world than to be in a classroom teaching kids about God! They are so young, enthusiastic, and innocent. I love it so much. It sounds strange, but I always feel like Jesus is sitting there in our circle on the floor, smiling at all these little faces.

—Lesley, Buffalo, NY

65

When I run I am happy. In my opinion, there is no better feeling than the rhythmic pounding of my feet against the pavement. The only limiting factor is my willingness to exert myself. It is an entirely unique freedom. I believe that true catharsis can be achieved only through the sweat and toil of a hard run. When I run I am oblivious to the world. Every step is a direct challenge against only myself. Everything achieved is the fruit my personal efforts. There is no pretext or excuse; the lucid truth alone is revealed. In this state of inner clarity, victory and defeat are relative. Only in my heart can the difference be distinguished. It is in this state that I am at peace.

—Joseph Larson, Danville, IL

An Unusual Birthday Gift

As another year quickly came to a close, I thought about the usual exciting things that go along with my birthday. What am I going to get? What am I going to do? Who am I going to invite?

I did something different though, something small but truly appreciated, and I didn't realize how much until someone told me. I remember feeling so good, and I felt such a light shine in me that all I wanted to do was give. It was an interesting feeling. I made a difference for someone else. It is not something that needed to be announced or praised, but the person I helped will embrace what I did and do it for others.

That is more happiness than any present could give me. The secret to happiness? Finding joy in other people's happiness. Seeing someone smile because of something I did is more rewarding than a trophy, more rewarding than recognition, because making someone else happy is a deep look into true happiness.

—Maria Mocerino, Los Angeles, CA

Many things in life can bring a person joy. For me it's snowboarding. Sure, people say it's a punk sport and only bad kids are into it, but that's not at all the case for me. Snowboarding is an escape. It's something I can do to get away from some problems and a way to spend time with my closest friends. But as I sit aloft a white, untouched snowfield, I also get this mix of exhilaration and awe. I can look at the surrounding mountains and see how beautiful God's creative landscape is. It also makes me think about where I stand in life. I clear my mind of all problems and think of everything that is good and important to me. Snowboarding is not only a sport but also an escape. The snow is a way of life to me: I learn new things and get the chance to think and to love.

—Josh Medcalf, Sublimity, OR

Happiness.

Resting my eyes after a long day's work, I sink into my bed and let the cozy mattress swallow me whole. A friend unexpectedly visits me, and together we eat a gallon of ice cream while watching classic movies. Receiving an awesome grade after long hours of studying, I smile contentedly, reaping the benefits of my hard work. Letting the glow of the spotlight warm my painted face, I hit the final note of my solo. My mom wipes away my tears after a stressful day at school. My dad congratulates me after my team wins a challenging game of baseball. Feeling intense words of emotion seep through my fingertips onto a piece of paper, I create a poem. Swimming, jumping, laughing, and screaming all invigorate me. I love my life and all who have made me the person I am today. Striving to win, dying to live, I experience pure joy through the routine and surprises of my everyday life.

—Brittany Bacon, Demarest, NJ

Things that make me happy

are my friends, my family, and my life. Waking up every morning is something that I think everyone should be happy and thankful for. Life is something that means everything to me, and I think everyone should appreciate it more than they do. Friends make me happy in the sense that they are always there for me, and I think it is great to know that there is always someone who cares and wants to listen. Family and God are the two things that make me the happiest. Even though my family can be hard at times, it is still one thing that I am very thankful for. God is awesome, and it is so good to know that he is always going to be there when I need him. Being happy is something that comes from love and compassion. Happiness, in my mind, cannot be expressed in words.

—Tim Spath, Riverhead, NY

What makes me happy? Interesting question, for not

many things accomplish that. I'm happy when I can get up, go to school, and know that at least one person will be overjoyed to see me. I'm happy when I talk to my three most trusted online friends because they like me for my personality rather than for my appearance. I'm happy when I make my parents happy. I'm happy when I do well on something I enjoy doing. I'm happy when I write and when people enjoy what I write. But most importantly, I'm happy when I feel accepted by people who don't even have to acknowledge my existence.

Not everyone can feel happy being, dare I say, single. I can guarantee that there is no male alive that can replace my list of favorites. Some come close, but without the above experiences, I wouldn't survive with or without a boyfriend.

—Christina Wand, Springfield, MO

What makes me happy are simply the things everyone

else takes for granted. Some of the things I am thankful for and that make me happy are parts of me. For example, my legs take me places and let me do things that make me happy. Places such as Niagara Falls and the Grand Canyon show me God's wonder and awe. Another thing that I am thankful for are my eyes. My eyes help me to see the places my legs take me, and seeing them makes me happy. I am thankful for my ears and sense of smell. With these I can hear the water of a waterfall and smell the salty air. The last thing I am thankful for that makes me happy is waking up every morning to use the other things that I am thankful for and to do the things that make me happy.

—Kevin Murphy, Chicago, IL

Many things make me happy. A beautiful sunrise, a couple in love, and a family playing together are just a few of these things. There is one thing that makes me happier than all the others. She is my little sister, Jillian. Jillian is a miracle child. She has diabetes, arthritis, and epilepsy, and she is only five. Every day she has a smile on her face because she knows she is special and God gave her special gifts. She does not concentrate on her disabilities but on her abilities. She is an inspiration to many, especially her family and friends. My little sister knows how to brighten everyone's day with her smile. Her smile and laugh are contagious. Jillian is my joy.

—Kaitlin Parlor, Omaha, NE

May people experience the fulfillment of happiness every day. What do you think makes you happy? Is it money? Is it friendship? What it is that really makes your heart feel at peace?

Love comes in many different forms, but love is what makes me happy. Love is a sign that tells me I am special to someone. Being loved unconditionally by someone is the greatest experience I can ever have. It makes me happy to know that the person who loves me is watching over me and listening to every word I have to say. Someone special expressed love to me in several different ways. Sometimes I didn't realize that his actions were out of love, until I lost him. Since that day, I have never lost the happiness in my heart because I know this person will always love me. I love you, Grandpa!

—Brandon, Detroit, MI

Why am I happy?

Maybe it's because
Jesus loves me,
Protects me,
Provides for me,
Watches over me,
Feeds me,
Guides me,
Stands beside me.
Maybe it's because
Jesus is my friend,
My advisor,
My consultant,
My energizer,
My idol.
Maybe it's because
Jesus gives me knowledge,
Gives me life,
Gives me strength,
Gives me power,
Gives me hope,
Gives me warmth,
Gives me shelter.
Maybe it's because
Jesus is in my life.
Maybe it's because
Jesus knows my mind.
Maybe it's because
Jesus is the way.
Better yet, it's because
With Jesus, I am saved.

—Solange Ealy, Jamaica Estates, NY

What makes me happy is playing basketball with my cousin. Even though she is a girl, I like paying with her because ever since we were little, she and I used to play all the time. I helped her get better at her game, and she helped me too but not that much. I'm still better than her!

—Keith Williams, Audubon, PA

There are many things in my life that make me happy. The one thing that pleases me the most, however, is doing the best I can at everything I do. No matter what it is, I always try to do my best. By doing this, I can take satisfaction in the fact that I've done all I can to make my life and the lives of those around me better. This is something that no one can take away from me, and that I can take comfort in knowing. The feeling of satisfaction that I experience through doing my best makes me happy. As long as I continue to try my hardest, I will be happy for the rest of my life.

—Matt Flanagan, Somerville, NJ

There are many things that make me happy. Out of the many, there is one special thing that makes me happy. That one thing is my family—more specifically my dad. My dad was diagnosed with cancer about two years ago. Ever since that day, I have always been with him. He became my best friend, along with my mom. I formed a close relation- ships with both my dad and my mom. Over the years, my dad has gotten worse. His condition isn't getting any better. As the times got worse, I started spending more and more time with my family.

The fact that my dad is getting worse is not what makes me happy. What makes me happy is his smile. Every morning before I leave for school, I always tell my dad that I'm leaving. He always smiles and says, "I'll be waiting for you." When I get home from school, I go straight to my dad. My dad never opens his eyes or smiles at anyone, yet when I come home from school and say, "Hi Daddy, I'm back," he finds the energy to open his eyes and smile. That smile is what makes my day. That smile is what makes me happy. That smile is the reason I want to go home as fast as possible. It is that smile that makes me smile and be happy.

—Hyun Joo Lee, Jamaica Estates, NY

Art by Gracie Stoltman, Winona, MN

My foot taps chronically as I hum along with a smile. My soul feels sympathy when I hear syrupy rhythms and bellowing intervals. I feel inclined to shout when the beat of a piece gets faster. Whether it is the lyrics or the song, my heart is dependent on music for an everlasting feeling of happiness. I see beauty in the sounds of heels clicking down a street with nonlinear rhythms. It is my tool for relaxation and motivation through life. Seeing others relate through music allows me to know that God put it here for a reason. I believe stories of people who were aided and healed by music because it is not only music that makes me happy but also its effect on others. Through music people can be healed and broken hearts can be sealed.

—Briana Lane, Los Angeles, CA

Art by Caitlin Bambenek, Winona, MN

I feel
most happy
when the ground is breaking,
the dark earth giving way to the
warmth of a yellow sun. I feel most
content when I breathe the cool air
and it runs through my little green
veins, giving life to my being.
I feel most at peace when
the gentle wind sways
my
vermilion
hair
and
makes
me
dance
in
the
warmth
of a yellow sun.
I feel calmed when the
morning dew trickles down my
emerald spine and collects in the
crevices of my broad
hands.
I
feel
most
loved
at
the
touch
of a young child, a gift to his
unexpecting mother. My growth ends, yet I live on in the eyes
of another. And I make them happy in the warmth of the yellow sun.

—G. M. I., Pontiac, MI

Singing and running are the things that make me happy. They help me grow as a **spiritual individual** and bring me closer to God.

—Lisa C. Dabrowski, Pontiac, MI

Happiness is contagious. You smile at someone, and they smile back. **The cycle repeats,** just like peace.

—Melissa Ortiz, Bronx, NY

Knowing that I **brought joy into someone's life** gives me peace of mind.

—John Anderson, Maysville, KY

Some people say that **money, cars, or, a big house** makes them happy, but not me. What makes me happy is **playing basketball** with my friends. Some may say it's just a game, but for me it's a lot more!

—Gabriel J. Almario, San Diego, CA

One of the things that makes me happy is **seeing people around me** trying to do what's right, making good decisions, and **trying to better themselves.**

—Albert R., Audubon, PA

The thing that makes me most happy is **waking up every morning** knowing that I am going to **live another day.**

—Annemarie Rutan, Indianapolis, IN

The thing that makes me happy is seeing others **enjoying themselves.** Happiness has a **domino effect.**

—Casey, Wilmington, DE

Happiness is going on an **unexpected quest** with one of my best friends or reading a tale that is filled with **illusion and action.** Happiness is venturing forth into a world that is **bound only by my mind.**

—Bernie J. Michael, Grosse Pointe Shores, MI

I find **peace and happiness** through art. It is a calming and therapeutic way to pass time, but it also can be a way to **express aggression, frustration, and sadness.** . . . I believe that satisfaction can be attained simply by creativity.

—Reyenne, Jamaica Estates, NY

Happiness in **interdependent.** . . . Knowing that your **simple act of kindness** helped to improve the life of a fellow human being is an **ultimate power.**

—Christina L. Johnston, Springfield, MA

What makes me happy is **being able to walk.** . . . I am happy to walk because one day in football practice, I got hit, was knocked unconscious, and had a seizure. I got the impression, lying on the field, that **I might not be able to walk again,** and I got scared.

—Danny Corbett, Mission Hills, CA

The greatest joy I've found is **my five-year-old sister, Claudia.** I always wanted a baby sister, and I consider her the ultimate prize.

—Sherlie Francois, Brooklyn, NY

What makes you happy? Why?

I would ask Jesus **how he feels about people who don't believe in him.** What happens to the people who never had the opportunity to learn of his existence?

—Cara Vallenti, Drexel Hill, PA

After September 11, 2001, the American reaction to those who look like Afghanis or anyone foreign-looking **was uncalled for.** After we had lost so many, **we hurt** so many more.

—Megan E. McDonald, Salt Lake City, UT

ABOUT OUR QUESTIONS

Jesus, when you were being crucified, is it true that **you did not feel any anger** toward the Romans who were persecuting you?

—Dominick Caggiano, Bronx, NY

Eventually I would ask one big question: **Do you love me, God?**

—Thuc Pham, Newton, MA

If I could sit down with Jesus and ask him any question I want, I would ask him why people, especially children, have to suffer. I understand that through suffering we can learn important lessons that can bring us closer to God, but how long must a person suffer? I mean, why does one person have to suffer so much? Couldn't we all suffer a little? It's so hard to watch children suffer over and over again. Each loss sets them back farther and farther, making recovery even harder. I understand the concept of learning through trials, and I know suffering can bring surrounding people closer to God as they learn to serve the one in need. I know we are children of God, and God aches for us when we are hurt, but how much is too much? When will my little sister see and walk again?

—Sarah Christine Connelly, Altoona, PA

The world, especially in today's day and age, is full of great injustices. People being stripped horrifically of their loved ones, and teenagers feeling depressed and miserable are everyday injustices people look past. I honestly cannot choose just one out of the world's many faults. All the problems that I see as great injustices, however, could be solved so quickly and so simply by love. If more people took the time to just view life in a positive manner, there would be so much less pain and hurt in the world. If the world's selfishness became selflessness, and if people thought about others, there would be less depression, suicides, homicides, fear, pain, sadness, and suffering. If those horrible men who flew the planes into our buildings had a heart and thought of the mothers, fathers, aunts, uncles, cousins, husbands, wives, brothers, sisters, sons, daughters, and friends who were so innocent, there would have been no pain and loss felt that horrendous day. It's hatred and overwhelming anger that cause the world's most critical problems, so in theory it could be counteracted by their opposites. I believe that small

Poverty is one great injustice that America overlooks too often, yet one I care about deeply. The great distinction between the few very rich and the many very poor strikes me as something we can all help erase. The issue hits those below the poverty threshold very hard, and even people like me, when I think about the children who are going to bed hungry, sleeping on the streets, and dying preventable deaths. Mothers are working their hardest but do not get paid enough to supply their families with the basic necessities. We can pray for these unfortunate people. More important, we can also write to our congressmen, organize job fairs, and actively contribute to the advocacy for better housing and living conditions for those who need it. Poverty is an issue that needs to be analyzed and eliminated before we can truly call ourselves the Americans our forefathers wanted us to be: the free, the liberated, and the proud.

—Mary Langan, Washington Township, NJ

gestures of love and peace could make the world smile together. We should all stand united, not just the United States of America, but all mankind. We're all in this life together.

Life is much too short to spend all of it hating. A little compassion could go a long way, and love could heal the wounds of war, bullying, and hateful crimes.

—Brandon Bosqué, South Amboy, NJ

I would ask Jesus: If man was made in God's image, why would he allow us to have the right to make wrong choices? I understand that people have free will, but if man was truly made in God's image, then we would not make wrong choices. We would always make right, Christian choices. Jesus would probably give me a divine, poetic answer to my question. I guess that's how God is sometimes.

—Joe Wells, Aumsville, OR

An injustice that I care about is our fight with Afghanistan. I understand that those who planned, supported, and carried out the plans should be punished, but many people want to punish an entire nation for the attack. Many people say the Afghan people are against us or that Muslims are against us, but that is not true. Many Afghanis and Muslims aren't against us. I know that a lot of Afghanis, especially women, would be more likely to be for us than for the Taliban, who is making their lives miserable. So why would we fight fire with fire and kill innocent people? We'll cause more problems, and more people will hate us. There are not really a lot of ways I can solve this, but I know that I do not have to help spread it. I will not blame certain people for what happened on September 11, 2001, or anyone who could be innocent anytime. Now we know that blame can kill.

—Andrea Watkins, Louisville, KY

If I could sit down with Jesus, I would ask him why our world is so messed up, and why people die every day.

I would tell him that I'm thankful for life, for my family, and for my girlfriend. I would ask him to give me better hopes and dreams. And if I could see God, I'd ask him to give me everlasting life.

—Albert Rodriguez, Audubon, PA

I personally see great injustices in the workplace for female employees. My mom has worked the same job for fourteen years and is at the same level of achievements as her fellow worker, but she still gets a lower salary. Some men in the plant are lower ranking and have less experience, but they get greater pay. Even the head of the plant treats my mom as an inferior. He has her do work that doesn't even pertain to her position. There's nothing right now that I can do to change this, but I can speak out when I'm older because I truly think that men and women

I would ask Jesus to try to lessen the hurt we sometimes have to endure. I know everything happens for a reason, but I would like him to know that when the World Trade Center was attacked too many people died. This tragedy was too much. I would like him to try to let us live a life with less heartache. I know Jesus does not give us more than we can handle, but I feel that this was so devastating. If he could possibly punish those who deserve to be punished and let us know that this was a wrong done to us, the people who attacked us will be held accountable for what they did.

Jesus knows what's best for us, but I would like to know from this particular incident what we have learned and how to accept what has happened. My heart was broken when this happened to our country, and I want Jesus to explain how we can learn from this horrible act of terrorism.

—Christine Jaccarino, Staten Island, NY

are created equal, especially in the job world. I've thought about it, and I believe that women often think more rationally about subjects pertaining to funds, ethics, and life in general than men do. Women and men should be treated equally, in business and in life.

—M. A. Baszis, Westville, IL

If I could sit down with Jesus and ask him a question, I'd ask him how the universe was created and why. How did everything that exists just come out of nothing? If nothing existed before the dawn of time, how did God even exist to create the world? Did God create only the world or did God create everything else too? Did the universe come into being with a purpose, or was it made just for kicks? If there are other planets with intelligent life, why is God paying special attention to this one? Is Jesus just making his rounds through the universe? Questions like these boggle my mind.

—Zachary Sarver, Anniston, AL

If I could sit down with Jesus, I would like to ask him why he allows evil to exist. If evil is destroying the beautiful world God created, then why not get rid of all evil? God is the creator of everything that exists in this world. He has the power to destroy anything he wants to as well.

When I was younger, I would get myself in trouble by questioning God's power. I would question whether or not God was as powerful as we were taught. I strongly believed that if God was as powerful as we thought him to be, then nothing evil could possibly exist. Looking around in our world, we see evil everywhere. We are taught that God puts temptations on this earth to test us. The world would be better if God totally destroyed all evil. It would be more peaceful if God destroyed evil.

—Lauren Achacoso Albano, Staten Island, NY

Then it came, a storm unlike any other. It was born of darkness and brought pain and suffering to all who came near it. It broke rocks and destroyed entire villages. Then out of the sky descended a light that shined on the darkness. The darkness was gone, and the sky was clear once more.

This is the story of the triumph of myself over the problems and hardships within me. I went through life with questions that no one answered. This void created fear that maybe God did not exist. With help from Jesus, I overcame my inner difficulties.

Night after night I prayed for answers. I asked my parents, my teachers, and myself, but I got no reply. I nearly lost hope that Jesus was there, but I knew in time I would fully accept God, or at least continue to pray until I had some answers.

—John O'Dell, Riverhead, NY

To me abortion is one of the greatest social injustices. From the moment of conception to natural death, all life is a sacred gift from God and shouldn't be taken away because it is convenient for one or both parties involved. It is murder.

I'm fifteen years old, and there aren't too many ways I can help solve this problem. The answer is definitely not blowing up abortion clinics or threatening, harassing, or killing the staff or women who attend these clinics. The people who do such things are going against what they are trying to preserve: life for all. I can help get the message out that there are other options, or when I'm old enough I can vote for politicians who are pro-life. All I'm sure of is that abortion is wrong and something needs to be done to eliminate this injustice.

—Emily Stefanov, Anniston, AL

One of today's greatest injustices is racism.

Living in New York City, I've witnessed many incidents of racism and discrimination toward people of color. This happens a lot when one lives in such a large city. To give an example, say four black males enter a store. Usually they are very closely watched from the time they enter the store until they leave.

There are many ways we can stop racism and change the way people of color are treated. People of color need to be appointed to government jobs and other positions where we can change things from within. We're outnumbering white people in all the wrong places, like state prisons instead of the Pentagon or the White House.

—Orane Sewell, Brooklyn, NY

If I could sit down and talk with Jesus, I would ask him why he didn't call women to be Apostles. I want to know if the reason he didn't call them was because he was afraid of what others might think. The only reason women can't be ordained (that makes sense to me) is because Jesus didn't call women to be his Apostles. His times were so different from ours. I completely believe that if Jesus lived right now instead of two thousand years ago, he would have called women. It just wasn't acceptable then.

I would also like to know if he thinks we are doing a good job today. Is this how he wanted the Church to be, or are we doing everything wrong? If he could come back and critique us, we would be better people in a better world.

The last thing I would ask Jesus is: How did you do it? How were you able to go through with your mission and Crucifixion? Starting a mission would be hard if you already knew the end result would be your death.

Lightning streaks across the sky. The thunder roars. I am at football practice as the storm sets in. The day has been long and challenging. I'm soaked with sweat and absolutely exhausted. Thirsty, hungry, and bone-tired, I press on. Finally, it's time for our water break. I trudge over to the water trough. Suddenly, I feel sensations of heat and a feeling of disorientation. My vision begins to blur and breathing becomes ever so hard. Pain spreads across my chest, and I can't breathe. I try not to show it, but I'm beginning to panic. As I drag myself over to the trainer through the treacherous atmosphere, the water pours down from the heavens. I long to shout, "Roll of thunder, hear my cry!" As I try to get help, I pray to God, begging him to save me and to let me live another day.

—Matthew John Rachwalski, Palos Hills, IL

That would be terrifying. Is the world as it is today worth all that? I know what his answer would be, but it would comfort me and support me a lot to hear him say, "Yes!"

—Carrie Jarka, Danville, IL

I see great injustices in the black and poor communities. One in every four black males goes to jail. That statistic is much lower for white males.

When poor people are convicted and go on trial, more often than not they cannot afford their own lawyer. They have to take the lawyer the state provides. A rich person in the same situation can afford a better lawyer and, therefore, has an advantage.

This issue is a very big problem in society today. We need to stop stereotyping African Americans. Police may not even realize they are doing it, but it is a major issue. Better state lawyers also need to be hired to represent those of lower incomes. Our law system has turned hypocritical. Everyone should be treated equal before the law.

—Sarah Rupp, McSherrystown, PA

If I were allowed the opportunity to sit down and ask Jesus a question, without a doubt I would ask him to clarify the entire idea of temptations of the flesh. I would like him to tell me what he thinks about many of the sexual issues that young men and women face on a daily basis.

I think the major issue that I would like him to explain to me would be whether or not self-gratification is acceptable in his eyes and if there are any explicit conditions. Some of the major rules or conditions that I would ask him about would be regarding hormone levels during puberty and the state of mind while performing these actions.

With these questions answered, I feel that many young people would have a much easier time maturing into adulthood.

—Glenn Bluemer, Palos Park, IL

If I could sit down with Jesus, I would ask him why he chose to give me so many tests in my life. Not like written tests but physical and emotional tests. Some examples of physical tests are being born prematurely or needing a heart transplant. My emotional tests are much more painful. Such tests are the deaths of twelve family members and friends. I know Jesus wouldn't give me anything I couldn't handle, but I just wish he wouldn't have given the tests to me so close together and so early in my life. I would also ask why he chose to make me relate to so many things that none of my friends can, like "what doesn't kill you only makes you stronger" or the way these tests have given me such different views on things that my friends think are totally crazy. Finally, I would ask him if all these tests are meant to prove something to me or if they are just supposed to make me stronger.

—Alicia Ann Lehman, Somerville, NJ

If I could sit down with Jesus, I would ask him two questions.

The first question would be where he has been all my life. I would ask him this because I have never felt his presence. I believed in his presence when I was younger, and I figured my parents knew what they were talking about. Then I got older and stopped believing because a lot of bad things happen in this world. Even when I was younger, I couldn't understand why a God whom I have heard such great things about could allow such things to go on. When I was younger, I would even try to pray and to reason with him, but I've never gotten a response. As I got older, I stopped praying, and things didn't change. So when people say God has a reason, I just say it's coincidence.

The other question I would have to ask is if it was my fault. Personally I wouldn't see it was, but I would have to ask anyway, just to see how we stand. I guess if he was cool about it, and we saw eye to eye, I would apologize.

These are the questions I would ask Jesus if I were to sit and talk to him. I honestly don't think that'll ever happen.

—Bill McCrea, South Amboy, NJ

Rumors are one of the most dangerous weapons brought into a school. They can be cold, life-shattering daggers stabbed into our backs at any moment. One of the injustices in high school is that kids are judged from rumors before anyone takes the chance to get to know them. Just because we've passed someone in the hall a few times doesn't mean we know him or her, nor does it give us the right to judge him or her.

I think that to solve this problem we need to stop making assumptions and start listening to one another instead of listening to rumors. We'll find that we're not that different, and many of us have the same problems. We should start helping one another instead of turning to abuse. Then we can come to the realization that stereotypes are often wrong. We might see that the jock, the nerd, the basket case, the rebel, and the princess can all get along.

—Barbara Janiszewski, Saint Joseph, MI

The injustice I think is one of the worst is abortion. In the dictionary, abortion is the loss of a fetus before it is able to live outside the womb. It is legal for an abortion to be done intentionally. In my opinion, this is a terrible thing that should not be allowed. I think a law should be passed that says abortions are no longer legal. It makes me feel sad that every day innocent babies are being killed. More people should consider adoption instead of abortion.

Last year, my class went to the March for Life in Washington, D.C. I was glad to see that so many people have the same idea as I do when it comes to abortion. Maybe someday we will have an abortion-free world, and more people will realize abortion is not the answer.

—Ryan Navarro, Altoona, PA

I personally see a great injustice in the way that mentally disabled people are treated. My brother, Jesse, has Down's syndrome. He is now twenty years old and has faced injustice his entire life. It breaks my heart over and over again when Jesse comes home from school saying a boy there made fun of him.

I know that if people knew these special kids, they would not be so prejudiced against them. I think what might help overcome this injustice is to get both the mentally disabled and the "normal" people together. We should try to form a bond between the two people. I understand that people may be a little scared or intimidated at first, but disabled people are some of the most loving and caring people you will ever meet. Hopefully in the future the injustice will stop.

—Jamie Rose, Philadelphia, PA

Art by Isaac Zafft, Goodview, MN

Injustices exist all over the world. However, I believe the injustices against women are of the greatest magnitude. Women have been discriminated against since the beginning of time. Throughout history, women have continually fought for equal rights and fair treatment in society.

Due to the evident problem of injustices against women, it is crucial that we make reforms so all people are treated as equals. The main aspect of reforming this atrocity involves educating the public. Our society needs to be taught from a young age the importance of treating people fairly and with respect, and not judging others by their gender, race, age, or any other factor.

Women need to realize their importance and the beneficial contributions they have made to the world. Women should never feel restricted because of their gender. We are all equal as human beings and should be treated as such.

—Jane Desmond, Dobbs Ferry, NY

Art by Reid Prosen, Winona, MN

If I could sit down with Jesus, I would ask him to tell a funny joke in order to break the tension. Then I would ask him a little about himself, specifically about the things not found in the Bible. For example, what was his most embarrassing moment? Did he have any nicknames? I would ask him if he could change his name, what would he change it to and why? These questions would all be in good fun, but then I would get to the more serious questions. I'd want to know what heaven is like. I'd also like to know how it is that everything in nature works so perfectly. Finally, I would ask him what his favorite thing on earth was when he was human.

—Kristen Hendrix, Reading, OH

Art by Kathy Sherman, Winona, MN

If I could sit down with Jesus and ask him a question, I would ask him WHY? This is a very generalized word, but that's what I would want to know. WHY are we here? WHY is there war? WHY are we challenged with sin? I would ask him WHY there is indifference and different perspectives. I would want to know our purpose. If our purpose is to serve the Lord, then WHY would he allow Satan to stumble into our paths? I would ask him WHY? and then allow him to interpret the meaning of the question. I would want to know how God's mind works, his rhymes and reasons. I would want to know WHY he does not manifest himself into our lives. I would ask him WHY we were given free will. I want to know WHY in order to gain insight, knowledge, hope, and most of all the meaning of the mystery.

—Shannon Lippner, Chicago, IL

Art by Emily Wilant, Winona, MN

Why did you pick me to be one of your children? I often wonder why I was chosen and if I am **living up to your expectations.**

—Crissy, Drexel Hill, PA

How did you do it? How did you **show love toward everyone,** even to those who turned completely away from you?

—Theresa Gallenstein, Maysville, KY

I want to believe that **Jesus** had a normal, carefree childhood. At what time in his life did he come to **know the magnitude** of his mission on earth?

—Amy Hutter, Aurora, IL

I would ask Jesus, **"Why is there death?"**

—Brittany P. Stith, Philadelphia, PA

Why are we here? **What should we want** from the short life on earth and the eternity in the afterlife beyond death? What is the **meaning of life?** With the knowledge of where I am going on this **neverending road,** I could know how to respond to God's plan.

—K. M. R., Riverhead, NY

Why have you not come back, Jesus, to **give us en-couragement** about who you are and where you will always be? **Where are you** when we feel trepidation and consternation?

—Andrea Azuaje, Bronxville, NY

If you could sit down with Jesus, what question would you like to ask him?

Where do you personally see great injustices? How would you begin to solve the one you are the most passionate about?

What motivates me to say no in doing something that I know is wrong are **my morals** and the tiny fact that someone referred to as "**Mom**" will eventually find out if a wrong action was done on purpose.

—Christina Wand, Springfield, MO

Now, when I start saying okay, I **stop and ask myself** if I want to fall into that ditch again. The answer I come up with is no.

—Teresa Irene Ciccaroni, Jamaica Estates, NY

ABOUT OUR
STRUGGLES

The storm would be finding the courage to **stand for Christ** when no one else will and to know **what God is calling me to be** instead of fighting against the call.

—Sean Winningham, Indianapolis, IN

There is a **price** attached to everything in life. To give in to temptation may well bring **brief pleasure** or exhilaration, but **in the end** will only cause mishap and regret.

—Richard Bradstreet, Watertown, NY

If Jesus were to calm a storm in my life, as he did in the storm at sea, that storm would be my asthma. I know that I cannot get rid of it, but I just want it to not be so bad. And the worst part is, no one knows. Sometimes I wish I had a disease that everyone knew about, that everyone understood. But asthma isn't like that. Everyone sees me talking and even laughing, so they assume nothing is wrong. But what they don't know is that there is a pain in my chest that does not go away. No one knows what a struggle it is for me. I can only wish and pray every single moment that I do breathe that God will make it bearable or at least calmer. This is the truth, as exaggerated as it might seem. Medicine doesn't work and neither does trying to control it. I want a release, even if it is for just one day. I want a day that I would be able to play soccer, swim in a race, or just run to meet my friend without feeling pain or anger or helplessness, only happiness and calmness.

—Julie Balthazard, Dobbs Ferry, NY

My parents just recently split up, and I have had trouble dealing with it. I'm living with my mom, and I don't see my dad all that much anymore. I have been hoping ever since my dad moved out that they would get back together and that we would all be a family again. This whole thing has caused problems between my brother, my sister, and me. This would be the storm that I wish Jesus could calm. There are some days I think my parents are getting back together and then there are days that it appears that they hate each other and never want to see each other again. I hope and pray that Jesus can calm this storm in my life.

—Justin M. Grossman, Magnolia, DE

When I am in a situation where I am forced to choose right from wrong, I think of my mom. She is a hardworking and determined woman. She works long hours to provide for my brother and me. Although I don't always appreciate it, I do love her for it. At my age I am constantly up against temptations and am forced to see the right thing to do. This isn't always easy; most of the time doing the right thing isn't cool.

When I am in these situations, I think of my mom, a single mother who has worked very hard to raise me and tried to give me all I wanted. If I were to do the wrong thing, I would fail my mother and ruin all that she has given me so far in this lifetime. I truly want her to see me as a mature and responsible adult. And by choosing right from wrong, I could very well show her my true feelings for what she does.

—Kylie Steinbugl, Altoona, PA

97

My mom is like a distant memory in my mind.
I try to remember when she wasn't lying in bed sleeping,
But nothing comes to me.
God decided her fate
And decided to take her for reasons unknown.
I prayed to God to save her,
But he didn't answer my prayer.
Now I have lost my mom
and all hope that God exists.

—Adam R., Audubon, PA

Dear God,

How are you? I am not so good right now. I just found out that my mom and dad don't want to be married anymore. God, why don't they love each other? Is it something I said or did? Maybe it is because my room is always messy. How come sometimes bad things happen? I thought you made everyone good. Did we mess it up down here? I try my hardest to be good and to teach my little sister too. I'm sorry that things don't always turn out well. Thanks for reading my letter. Say hi to Grandma and my dog, Sherman, for me.
Love, Vickie

—Vickie Martinez, San Diego, CA

The storm in my life that would be cured would be the one between me and my parents. I am sixteen years old and just recently received my driver's license, which is causing constant warring between us. We are constantly arguing about curfews, driving privileges, and which people I can hang out with. There is hardly ever a peaceful moment. I do not see why my parents cannot let go a little. I hope and pray to Jesus every night that some event in either my life or my parents' will come through and calm the storm between us.

—A. J. K., Finneytown, OH

The Church teaching I find most difficult to follow is honoring parents. One reason it is difficult is because they think they're always right. They get stubborn when you try to prove them wrong. We are all just humans and can easily lose our temper.

Another reason is because we are young and want to try new things. However, parents set rules and restrain us from doing things. When we are punished for disobeying, sometimes we feel more anger towards parents.

It is also difficult to honor parents when they don't set good examples for their children. We understand that they are human, but it does lead us to lose respect for our parents when they do things like getting a divorce.

However, it is completely necessary to obey and honor parents because they gave us life and they love us and care for us deeply; everyone regrets disobeying and dishonoring parents.

—Martha Ksepka, Brooklyn, NY

A great storm in my life was the period of time when my mom and dad passed away. This happened in a period of two years. First, my father was diagnosed with cancer in 1998. This was a great transition in my life. My father stopped working, and my mother was supporting the family. My father died on January 10, 1999. It was the longest year of my life. I was always depressed. I tried to keep my mind off of it by doing things like cleaning and playing video games.

But it was not long before I heard about my mom having cancer, and I thought about the worst. A year later, it happened. If it weren't for the Church and the prayers said for me, I wouldn't be here right now. This was the storm in my life. It's been a long process, but with counseling and— most importantly, Jesus—I can live a normal life.

—Thomas Miller, Brooklyn, NY

I just lost someone very close to me. When she passed away, I made a silent promise to myself and to her that I would live life to its fullest and try to not do things I might regret. When I am tempted to do something wrong, something I will regret, I think of that promise and that special someone that the promise is for, and I just can't bring myself to do that wrong. I feel her presence with me, and I know she is in heaven looking down on me, acting as my guardian angel. She is such an important part of my life, and I feel horrible thinking about her watching me do wrong. She was always so understanding and sweet, and somehow I don't see myself doing anything that I know is wrong in her presence, which is still very much with me.

—Kristin Elia, Ringwood, NJ

In this time of hope and despair,
When you think that no one cares,
It helps to know the Lord is always there.
In times good and bad,
The things in life that make you sad,
When life is too hard to bear,
It helps to know the Lord is always there.
In times of love and hate,
The things we do that decide our fate,
When life isn't fair,
It helps to know the Lord is always there.
In this time of hope and despair,
We know there's someone who really cares.
It helps to know the Lord is always there.

—Carl Raymond Pawsat, Maysville, KY

One of the Church teachings
I find most difficult to follow is to turn the other cheek when someone hurts you. It is human nature to want to get revenge on a person who hurts you. You may not be able to control your feelings, but you can control how you react to the situation. Of course you're going to want to get revenge, but it is how you act on your feelings that matters. Before you do something, you need to think about the consequences of your actions. When you feel the need to get revenge because you are hurt, think about the pain you will bring the person who hurt you. Remember how much pain his or her action caused you. You don't want that person to be in pain either. It takes a lot of courage to do this, but if you ask God for help, he will give you the strength to conquer this cross.

—É. H., Seattle, WA

The storm in my life
that I would have Jesus calm would be the one containing the stress and busyness that I deal with every day. I feel that I let myself get too stressed out about accomplishing school assignments so that I can get good grades and in hopes of being accepted into a good college. As this suggests, I find myself looking ahead to the future too often. I normally fail to live each day to the fullest. Instead, I live my days in preparation for the future. This causes me to lose focus on what is really important in my life because I get too busy with looking ahead. I also lose sight of God in the midst of all this. I can honestly say that my life would be much better if my storm of stress and busyness was calmed.

—Brandon, Cincinnati, OH

The act of forgiving is the most difficult Church teaching to follow. Forgiving is not always easy. When someone hurts you in some way, it is the obligation of a Catholic to forgive. We are taught to love one another as Jesus loves us. But anger can get in the way of our obligation, and overcoming those feelings is quite a challenge. We should always turn to God and prayer for reconciliation.

In certain situations, such as rape, incest, or a murder of a loved one, it is nearly impossible to forgive. However, Jesus taught that if we do not forgive others, our Father in heaven will not forgive us. To many this may not mean anything because of the anger inside them. As Catholics, however, we should at least pray to find the strength within ourselves to be able to forgive.

—Elsa Best, Hoboken, NJ

Currently, the storm that I would ask Jesus to calm is the one of doubt and confusion regarding college. At this time in my senior year of high school, all my college applications are finished. Now I sit eagerly waiting for the mail to arrive each day, waiting for the envelope that will seal my fate. Once it arrives do I dare open it and be rejected? I am fearful of what happens if all the colleges say no. On the other hand, if more than one says yes, then I face the difficult decision of choosing one. Jesus, at this time I lack the faith and the knowledge to be positive that my decisions in regard to college are correct. Will you please help me stay on the right track and guide me in this difficult decision process?

—Justin J. Santolli, Oyster Bay, NY

I'm not usually tempted to do wrong. That's a once-in-a-blue-moon kind of thing. But when I am tempted, I don't find it hard to say no. I just stick to my guns and say, "You all can do that without me." There were times I gave in and did wrong, but as I get older, I get wiser.

When I am tempted, I just remind myself that God is watching my every move. I try to tell myself that there are requirements for heaven. For example, I was hanging out with friends one day, and we walked into a store that sold cool pens that my other friend bought earlier. They decided that we should steal them because they cost too much. I told them I wasn't down with that because God is watching.

—Janelle Cornelius, Brooklyn, NY

When I am tempted to do something wrong, I think about three things. I think about the ideals that I've had imprinted on my mind about sex, drugs, and alcohol by my parents and teachers and how disappointed they would be if I made immature decisions. I think about my friends and how they would look at me differently for acting in a juvenile way and wrecking someone else's life in the process. I also try to make the right decisions by considering the consequences of my actions. For instance, before pursuing a sexual relationship, I think about my boundaries and how my education about STDs, pregnancy, and abortion discourages me from going too far in a sexual relationship. If the negative consequences outweigh the positives, I am motivated to say no.

—Michael Weber, Cincinnati, OH

When I look into the darkness,

It's so empty and so alone,
A place so full of devastation
Where hidden truths do moan.
I reflect on my past
And see my weary ways,
Undermined memories of good and bad
That mesh to create this haze.
But as I reflect on the mistakes,
I see what I've done wrong.
Inspiration then motivates me
And keeps my spirit strong.
Now when I'm faced with difficulty
And tempted to choose the wrong path,
I reminisce on how awful I felt,
When a faulty decision left me with aftermath.
My inner strengths and medial influences
Play a role in my decisions each day.

There is no finite answer to what motivates me to do

right from wrong. I suppose it would be a mixture of factors that form
one resulting action. My motivation is something deep within me, much
more important than other people's opinions and my personal reputation.
It is an impetus deep within my heart that tells me to do the right thing.
It is the morality that was bestowed on me from my family and friends. It
is my consciousness that guides me to live the life of Christ. It is for my
parents who spent my entire life raising me ethically, honorably, and with
integrity. It is for myself that I may become one with the Lord to make
this world a slightly better place.

—Andrew J. Hajduk, Chicago IL

They help me distinguish between good and bad
And instill in me a little way.
I now know how to say no and see
I can follow the path
That God placed before me.

—Allison Gehring, Cincinnati, OH

Right now for me the storm in my life is about drugs. I found out a friend of mine is using them, and he drinks too. I wish that Jesus could help this person.

Now my problem is one of trust because it seems like my friends all have the risk of taking drugs, and this makes me worry. We just started a chapter about it in health class, so I know all the risk factors, and they are showing up more and more in my friends. I wish Jesus could stop this from always popping up in my head. I wish that he could help my friends with this problem.

—Jaclyn D. Ready, Albany, NY

Being a teenager in today's world gives you ample opportunity to deviate from the morals you have grown up with. Temptation is everywhere—from MTV to parties. It is impossible to hide from. Temptation's lure can be impossible to withstand, especially when you feel like all your friends succumb to it on a daily basis. The only comfort available to me in times of great doubt and temptation is the confidence I have in God and myself. I know I have a lot to stand for, and throwing it away for a mere indulgence that lasts only a moment could ruin or stain the rest of my life's hopes. I also always have the comfort of knowing that when I stand up against temptation, God will be there to support me.

—Benjamin Manthey, Dallas, TX

When I am tempted to do something wrong, my parents usually motivate me to say no. For example, when I am tempted to have sex, I always think about the consequences, which are getting pregnant, getting kicked out of my warm and loving home, and destroying my future and goals. What also motivates me is the young teenage girls who are pregnant or have a baby. They tell me that I should wait until I am ready emotionally and physically. Most important, they tell me to wait until I finish school and start my career. These young mothers tell me it's not worth rushing into because as soon as the baby is born, there is no time for me.

I must admit that temptation is hard to ignore, but I always have people surrounding me to snap me out of making that serious decision of having sex.

—Tiffany Marie Mendez, Bronx, NY

When I am tempted to do something wrong, the one thing that usually motivates me to say no is the grace of God. Someone once told me that when Satan is tempting me to do something wrong, I should just pray: "Jesus, I am weak. You need to make me strong."

You can never overcome temptation alone; you need God to help you. I believe that when we put aside all our pride and realize that we are broken before God, he will help us, and we will grow. This is the one and only way that I have found it possible to overcome temptation. When you ask Jesus for help in a humble way, he runs to your rescue because it is by the wounds in his hands, feet, and side that we are saved from sin and death.

—Jason J. Schumer, Perryville, MO

"You shall love the Lord your God with all your heart . . . and your neighbor as yourself" (Luke 10:27). Every Sunday I ask the Lord's forgiveness, and I promise to try harder to obey this teaching. Fifteen minutes later, I'm demanding that my sister get off the phone so I can call my friend! If it were Jesus himself standing there, I would never be so impolite and selfish. I forget that he is there. He is in the face of the sister I'm cranky toward, the friend I ignore at school, the parent I take for granted, and the teacher I gossip about. Loving all people means being considerate, forgiving, and having self-control. It's much easier to think about being nice in church and then to forget about it for the rest of the week. I have to realize that my mean actions hurt other people and that I should make the conscious day-to-day decision to change them.

—G. Riley, Morristown, NJ

When temptation comes my way, it is not difficult to know the right thing to do. What is hard, however, is to have the will and the courage to make the right decision by saying no. The foremost thing that motivates me to say no is a little thing called consequences. I am the kind of person who will always overanalyze a situation. If I conclude that an end result will hurt me in any way, I try to stay away from it. Even if I knowingly end up doing something that would hurt me, I would probably be worrying about the consequences the whole time. Despite the decision I make, I would not be able to enjoy myself either way. Worrying about an outcome is always a smart thing.

—Ross Albenice, Somerville, NJ

In Luke 8:22–25, Jesus calms a storm at sea. The storm can be compared to problems in life. There was a young girl. She never really understood life. She never knew the importance of family. She fought with her brother all the time. She didn't entirely obey her parents. Her father was hardly ever home. She took advantage of the simple things in life, never realizing how special they were. God was a small part of her life. It was as if he were asleep in her life just as Jesus was asleep on the boat.

One day something happened, and the girl woke up. Her parents were getting divorced. She never realized how much she loved her family until that day. Her parents were like the winds and waves in the sea. They created a storm. She realized that her life was falling apart and called out to the Lord for help, just as the Apostles called out to Jesus. Jesus calmed the storm at sea. The wind and waves subsided. The Apostles were awed. But this young girl still waits for Jesus to calm her storm. The wind and waves still quarrel and never stop. Her life is continuing to fall apart, but

I have done many wrong things in my life, things that hurt me and things that hurt others. Over the years of doing these bad things and making wrong decisions, I have found that you never get away with doing something wrong. You always get caught, maybe not physically, but inside yourself you have been caught. Everything I have done wrong in life, I have been caught. It doesn't feel good. I think about what my parents would say if they knew what I did. Making wrong decisions never leaves you. Everything wrong I have done in life I could put in exact order, how it happened, and whom I was with. I could also tell you how I felt. Being caught is the worst feeling.

So now when I want to make a wrong decision, I think of my past, I think of my parents, and, most of all, I think about myself.

—Name withheld, Seattle, WA

she is learning how to bring it back. She continues to grow closer to God each day. Her family is the most special thing to her. She no longer takes for granted the simple things in life. Maybe Jesus is calming her storm.

—Katherine Anne Levering, South Amboy, NJ

I have been a virgin for seventeen years, and I think that keeping my virginity is more difficult than losing it. The other day a boy told me that no girl my age could still be a virgin.

I have been so close to losing my virginity because I have been asked a million times by the opposite sex. Most of the time, the people who have lost theirs make up excuses to justify the act. They say their marriage would be garbage, and they want to know how to do it before they are married. Every day I pray that I can control whatever happens to my body. I don't want to lose respect for myself and the principles I hold.

—Kalifa Wright, Brooklyn, NY

When I am tempted to do something wrong, the thing that motivates me to say no is the thought of what may be the consequence of my action. If it is a larger issue, I think about how it will affect me for the rest of my life. I know that I am at a critical time in my life, and one bad decision could lead to severe consequences in the future. My choices may influence whether I get accepted to the college of my choice or whether a company will hire me when I am looking for a job. If I do something wrong, it may reflect badly upon my parents, who have given me every opportunity I could ask for. For this I feel I owe them respect, and one way I can repay them is to show that they have raised a son they can be proud of.

—Richard E. Karnia, Chicago, IL

In our lives we have many storms,

These fears we have that last so long,
But Jesus asks us where is our faith?
Our faith is overcome by our fears.
If Jesus could calm a storm,
A storm I've felt for so long,
I'd ask him to help me overcome my fear of rejection,
A fear of mine which needs reflection.
My fear is from the faith I lack,
But my emotions remain intact.
I want to be successful every day
But feel I'm not good enough to have my way.
Often I'm left feeling down,
I begin to feel no one's around.
I must learn that Jesus is with me, that I am me,
And that there is no such thing as pure perfection.
The only way my storm will calm is if I have a helping arm.

In my own life, I find the saying "Love your enemies" to be the most challenging to carry out. In nearly all aspects of life these days—school, work, sports—everything is driven by competition. Opposite sides on a sports team are no longer friendly rivals. By the power of competition, the sides are now despised enemies. Consequently, our world has become centered on one person trying to out do another. And with such an outlook on society, it is difficult to climb out of the claws of society, the claws of competition. In my life, I strive to be the best that I can be. But, in the atmosphere I have been raised in, those better than me are my enemies. Thus to follow Jesus' message to love your enemies requires you to separate yourself from society's views, which is not an easy task.

—Donald, Cincinnati, OH

Jesus is with me in everything I do;
Faith is the answer I must pursue.

—Alicia Marie Leo, Staten Island, NY

I believe that going to confession is difficult to follow. Even though I often go, I sometimes wonder about it. I think about how if God sees everything you do and what mistakes you make then why must you go through a priest to tell God. Sometimes it is hard to admit to your mistakes or tell someone that you have done something wrong. I feel talking to the priest makes you feel as if you have cleansed your soul.

Sometimes an insecurity that I have is that the priest is judging what I am saying. Although this is not true I feel that way.

In conclusion, I believe that because God is around you and with you wherever you go, going to confession is really just to be clear of your sins, not to tell God what you may have done.

—Ashley Deitchman, Washington Township, NJ

111

Since that unforgettable September day,

I have not been able to find a way in my heart to forgive those responsible for the attacks. They have destroyed the lives of thousands of people. The loss of spouses, parents, children, and friends can never be filled. How can I forgive the terrorists for such life-changing acts against these people? How do I forgive them for changing mine? Some say, "An eye for an eye, a tooth for a tooth." But that is not what Jesus teaches us. He told us to love our enemies and pray for them.

For these reasons, forgiveness is going to be one of the most difficult teachings for me to follow for many years. Until I learn to forgive easily again, I will try to put the thought of forgiveness into my mind. But I can see it will not be in my heart any time soon.

—Ryan Thomas Black, Dallas, TX

If Jesus were to calm a storm in my life, it would be the storm between my mom and me. One of my greatest wishes is to find out who my mother is. She is a mystery I must solve before I can create a complete identity as a woman in this world. My mother and I have known each other forever, yet it feels like we haven't even said hello yet. Her eyes tell a million stories, but she is like a deep unreachable well that holds old secrets in the dark. I know my father hurt my mother with a devastating intensity when she was young, and consequently, her heart was crippled for life. She couldn't show me love, and she couldn't show pain. Despite all that, I turned out with an incandescent heart full of love. I can only guess that if I didn't learn how to love, it must be an innate treasure she blessed me with. That makes her a truly beautiful person I wish to understand one day.

—Ramona Diebaté, Burien, WA

The Church teaching that I find most difficult to follow is the sacrament of Reconciliation. When I go to confession, I find it embarrassing to talk with a priest, especially one whom I know well. I feel that whatever I say will be committed to the priest's memory. For example, in my elementary school, I knew the priests of the parish very well and saw them on a daily basis. If I were to confess to chewing gum and sticking it under a desk, the priest would be watching me and my desk for the rest of school year.

The confessional itself is cramped. Once the priest recognizes you when you walk in, why should he sit behind the screen? I am a very private person, and I would rather discuss my sins privately with God. The Church requires the sacrament of Reconciliation, so I will continue going to confession despite my personal feelings. I must admit that I purposely choose a priest whom I don't know personally.

—Charlie, West Islip, NY

What kind of storm, exactly, would be brewing in a seventeen-year-old girl who lives in a quiet suburban town, attends a prestigious private school, and receives A grades that needs to be calmed by Jesus? I do not sleep in the cold on a bench as the homeless are forced to do; I am not hungry for food.

However, I hunger for balance in my life. The pressure to receive higher grades, to do well in my advanced placement and honors courses, and to keep up with cross-country running, kungfu, and horseback riding builds up. A stress storm appears as a series of arguments with my college-driven mom, as nervous breakdowns, and as tears. Sadly, I am focused on molding my life into the perfect college transcript. So, my prayers to Jesus are to awaken in my life a purpose to be satisfied and proud of, not a purpose to make the grade.

—Karen Tam, Newton, MA

113

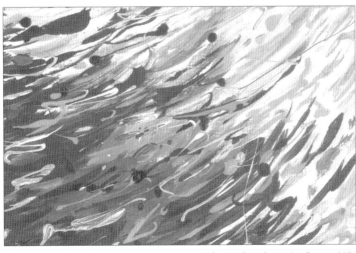

Art by Andy Palmer, La Crosse, WI

I would want Jesus to calm the **confusion in my life** so that I could see clearly and maybe even **choose a path** that is right for me.

—Michelle Ann Martini, Newton, MA

I am motivated by sports. Because I wouldn't want to do wrong and **put my gift** of athletic ability **in jeopardy,** I am motivated to say no when I am tempted.

—Alex J. Dickinson, Watertown, NY

It is really **hard for me to believe** women are not capable of being priests. Women can have **as much effect** on people as any man.

—Katie, Little Rock, AR

If Jesus could calm a storm in my life, I would ask him to **take away the pain** I have every day from **not having my mom** with me.

—Corrie, Hermitage, PA

Did you ever think your life could build up such an enormous and threatening storm? Well, in my busy life, the storm is almost ready to destroy my faith. Often **I don't even get time to pray.**

—Nicky Dumond, Tyngsboro, MA

When you are tempted to do something wrong, what usually motivates you to say no?

If Jesus were to calm a storm in your life (as he did in the story of the storm at sea in Luke 8:22–25), what would that storm be?

Which Church teaching do you find most difficult to follow? Why?

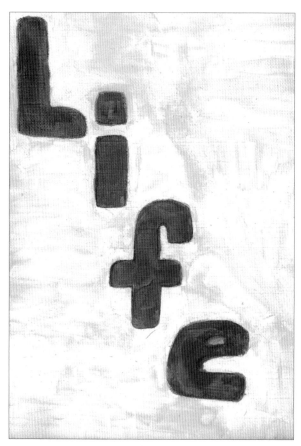

Art by Dustin Pozanc, Winona, MN

Boys, when you don't want to be with a girl any longer, please **explain it** to her in **any other way** than an instant message.

—Karen, Cincinnati, OH

I want my husband to be **modeled in the image of Jesus.** But, of course, there needs to be a romantic side to him.

—Christina Clarke, Drexel Hill, PA

ABOUT
EACH OTHER

Men have emotions just as women do. Men don't like to **show their emotions** because we think that **letting them show** will make us look feminine.

—Jacob Marganski, Rossville, IL

I will **be with my family** at all challenging times and when they need me most. If my wife and I are having problems, we will **get guidance** so that our kids don't have to go through their parents' divorce like I had to.

—Thomas M. D'Angelo, South Amboy, NJ

Sometimes boys tend to be a little sexist and have no feelings toward females. For example, I was talking to this boy, and when I told him that I play basketball, his comment was: "That is really funny, a girl who plays basketball. That sport is meant for boys only." When I heard this, I was a little hurt but it also made me strive to do better so that I could show him that basketball is not only for boys and that girls can also be good in sports. Although this boy is the first one who said it, later some of my "friends" who are also boys told me things like, "You should drop out," or "Girls shouldn't play ball." I wish boys understood that it is really hard for a girl to succeed in something that was originally meant for boys, and when they say things like that, it really tears us down.

—Syisha Archbold, Newton, MA

"The most important part of a relationship is communication." But if males do not understand what you are saying, we can't fulfill this relationship. Whether you are a wife, girlfriend, mother, or sister, it is almost as if you speak in code. We never understand things the way you would like us to. For guys sometimes it can be a guessing game as to what you want us to do. For example, say a guy's wife or girlfriend is mad at him, and she says, "I don't want to talk to you." This is where the typical male gets confused. Are we supposed to try to talk to you anyway to comfort and settle you, or are we supposed to obey your wish? Therefore, females must understand that males are not trying to be mean, rude, or unsympathetic. We do our best to fulfill your needs, but we sometimes have a hard time understanding the message.

—Christopher A. Suffoletto, Hamburg, NY

Gender equality is a nice thought. Unfortunately it is not yet a reality, though it is closer to being so in the United States than in other parts of the world. This truth makes it really hard to be a girl in this world where men are exalted on high all the time. It is men who control governments. There may be a few women in politics, but the ratio of men to women is in no way comparable. Women athletes do not receive half the attention male athletes get. The only women who are really noticed are the Hollywood starlets. The message seems to be that only beautiful women are worth noticing. Women should be congratulated on their strength, their presence of mind, and their intelligence. The archaic belief that women are merely decorative needs to be shattered and replaced with the image of a capable and compassionate human being.

—Christine Cornwall, Philadelphia, PA

Sometimes when talking to girls, I get the impression they believe that all guys look for is sex. Girls seem to think guys want them just for their body and that's all. To me, that is insulting. Sadly, some guys do think that way, but not all do. I am seventeen years old, and I have never had a girlfriend. I will be more than ecstatic when I am finally blessed with that first relationship, but it won't be because of the sexual aspect of it. I will be excited because then I will have someone to dance with at school dances, someone to hold during a sad movie, someone to be on the phone with at two in the morning on a Saturday night, and someone to tell how beautiful she is and how lucky I am every time I see her. Girls need to know we are all not sex-hungry pigs. I try my hardest not to be, and I know others do too.

—Thomas Biondo, Detroit, MI

I wish that men knew that not all women are sensitive I hate being stereotypically dubbed as a wimp who cries over everything. I am not saying that I do not have feelings, but I do not cry over dead animals, movies, or stuff that might make someone else cry.

Women are strong and capable, but no one seems to understand my point of view when I say that women have the willpower to do almost anything. I don't think that people realize how many women are behind the decisions concerning our nation. It bothers me to know that with all our strength, people still see this as a male-dominated society. I just want others to see the benefits of having women as leaders and not see them as just sensitive wimps.

—Katrina L. Gerding, Scio, OR

How many times have you heard a woman say, "Why are men such jerks?" "Why can't men just share their feelings?" "Why is it hard for a man to say I love you?" or "Why can't men be more sensitive?"

These are just a few questions I've heard women ask. I hope that women realize that not all men are jerks and not all men are the same. Once women get to know us personally, they will understand that we can be sensitive people too. Of course, when you first meet a guy, he is more than likely going to try and be something he is not.

There are a few things a girl should know about men when dealing with a relationship. Most women wonder why we never share our feelings. I honestly don't think we really know how we feel. We have too much going through our minds at once, and we get frustrated mentally and lose track of our thoughts. Unless we have some major problem bothering us, such as depression or the loss of a loved one, we have no idea what to feel. For example, it is really hard for a man to say "I love you," especially for the first time. Either we are not completely sure what to think, or we feel forced to say something and then get scared. Women want us to be more sensitive, but to a man a little sensitive is too sensitive, and they no longer feel like a man.

Impressing girls is simple.

Boys, here are ten things you can do to impress a girl:

10. Communicate with her about things you do.
9. Tell her that she's beautiful, not hot or fine.
8. When you say you are going to call, CALL!
7. Do nice things like hold her hand in public, even around your guy friends.
6. Remember the little things that she says because when your chance comes, you'll impress her by showing that you listen to what she says.
5. Always respect a girl by telling her the truth; she will find out if you lie, so you may as tell the truth.
4. Never brag to your buddies about something personal to her.
3. Always remember dates like her birthday and big anniversaries.
2. Don't say I love you if you don't mean it.
1. When a girl gives you her heart, try not to break it. Once it is broken, it is hard to piece it back together again.

—Christina Hengtgen, Seattle, WA

Unless a man has settled down with a girl for a few years, most men don't want a relationship. It is especially hard for a man in his teens, because he is too young for a long-term relationship. I think a lot of men in their teens fear commitment because of the stress that comes along with it. For all the women out there, take these facts into consideration the next time you go out and settle down with a guy.

—Christopher M. Wojcik, Harper Woods, MI

Everybody has an idea of his or her future life partner or true love. Every individual has unique personality traits that make him or her a very gifted person. My idea of a future partner is a girl who can be very playful and funny. That is my kind of future life partner.

I also dream or wish that my true love will be someone who is smart, talented, and beautiful, both inside and out. My future life partner is somewhere out there in the world, and she is probably thinking the same way I am thinking. I await her arrival, and I hope she turns out to be the way I think and dream she can be.

—Don Anthony Rana, Brooklyn, NY

I wish people of the male gender understood the emotional needs of females. Women show a lot more emotion than men do. It would be great if men could demonstrate more understanding of the female's initial feelings. Typically, men try to solve a problem when it would be best to simply stop and listen with compassion.

Men also misunderstand a woman's physical strength. Males and females should be treated equally, especially in sports. Men often underestimate a woman's potential. There should be no gender differentiation regarding sports. All athletes deserve fair opportunities and respect that is based on their performance rather than their gender.

—Alexandra Lee VanHull, Saint Chair Shores, MI

What I wish males knew about females is that we are not as society portrays us to be. For example, we are not to be treated without respect because of all the music videos that make woman look low class by acting improper and wearing revealing clothing. Many women are not like that. Just because one woman does something wrong

I've been asked many times what my dream girl would look like. What color would her hair or eyes be? What dress size would she wear? However, when I think about the woman with whom I will spend the rest of my life, there is no ideal look. I have no idea what I want that person to look like because I have not met her yet. In other words, my ideal woman is only a voice I hear. I hear bits and pieces when I imagine different things we would do together. Most important, she must be fun and happy to be with me. I want a girl I don't have to hide my true self from. She can be just as crazy as I can be. I'm already tired of acting like something I'm not to impress a girl. I wish I could be with a woman who is beautiful on the inside, not just on the outside. That's the kind of woman I imagine going to bed with every night.

—Greg Viglione, Hamburg, NY

should not give all women a bad reputation. So what I want the male gender to know about women is do not judge us because of what's shown in the media, and do not stereotype women.

—Jennifer A. Freire, Hoboken, NJ

Ideal men are good only for standing on pedestals and serving as models for sculptors. This is why I hope that my future life partner has faults—not too many, but enough so that I don't have to feel overly self-conscious of my own.

I hope he has trials in his life. I wish for him to lose sometimes so he may learn to do so gracefully and to treasure his triumphs all the more. I wish for him to be betrayed so he learns the importance of commitment and keeping promises. I hope the road of life for him is bumpy so he will learn perseverance. My wish is that he will learn important lessons from all these things and not let them leave him without hope or faith. Most of all, I pray that I will be worthy of him whenever he comes along.

—Emily Michaelson, Watertown, NY

My hope for my life partner is that she be somebody with whom I can share the gift of life in every sense of the word. My dream is to have someone by my side who is not only my partner but also my best friend. She will be someone I can completely trust with my life, no matter what the circumstances. I hope to have someone with me who will love me for who I am. I will need someone I can rely on, but also, someone who can rely on me with complete faith in me. I pray that my life partner is someone who can correct me if I make a mistake and who will bring out the best in me. Most important, I hope my life partner is someone whom I can love with my entire heart, body, and soul.

—G. P. T., Middleton, CT

A Prayer for My Future Life Partner

I pray that you are forever at peace with the world, but, more important, that you always stay at peace with yourself. I pray that you are always able to see the beauty that exists all around us and the beauty in yourself. I pray that you are always able to recognize who you are and that you are able to accept what you are. I pray that no matter how old you become, you are always young at heart. I pray that you never look at someone for what they are, but you always see them for what they are capable of becoming. And most important I pray that you are forever loved and forever able to love.

—Anne Carroll, Indianapolis, IN

I really wish that girls would see what I find to be true.
Guys aren't sex-crazed maniacs looking for some fun.
Why can't they see the serious side, where all the work is done?
We really aren't stupid; most of us understand
That when someone is down, they need a helping hand.
We can listen and have conversations too.
And our egos aren't hard to push through.
Not all guys want to destroy and bomb everything.
To some of us, life is a very sacred thing.
God helps our faults, our convictions, and us all.
Everyone should be responsible for his or her own actions.
I must admit that sexes are different.
But that shouldn't stop what I find to be true—
God loves us the same amount as you.

—Steven Cosgrove, Magnolia, DE

To My Future Husband

Every girl dreams of meeting the perfect guy, falling madly in love with Prince Charming, and riding off into the sunset to live happily ever after. Realistically, however, these fantasies are often met with broken hearts, empty promises, and the shattered dreams of a girl too naive to realize that her expectations of her partner are so specific and cliché that she will never be able to truly love him. I realize a girl must have some standards and not settle for anything less than her one true love, but I also know that love comes in unexpected ways. I have only one absolute requirement for my future life partner: love me. That's it. But love all of me with all of you. Show me a love that sustains me, feeds my soul, and nourishes my spirit. For with love comes joy, respect, and sacrifice. Love is the key to everything.

—Carrie A. Causino, Saint Louis, MO

My life partner would be someone I get along with very well and a person I can share a common bond with. She would be someone I have known for a while and have developed a great friendship with. I hope she is somewhat intelligent; I would rather not have an airhead for a wife. She would be a person with whom I could share any secret and would not feel embarrassed.

The thing that is most important to me is that we would love each other very much. She would be someone very special and dear to me. This person would always be true to me, and I would be the same. We would both have a great sense of humor and would be able to laugh and joke together. We would be secure enough to trust one another in any situation, and we would honor one another in our own ways.

Looks are not the most important thing to me, but I would like her to be beautiful, or at least beautiful in my opinion. We would be a couple that could help each other out in a bad situation. She would be someone who could comfort me when I'm sad. I don't want the smartest or the most beautiful in the world, all that matters is that I love her and she loves me. Money doesn't mean a thing because it can't buy happiness.

—M. S., South Amboy, NJ

I can remember putting a pillowcase over my head, pretending it was a veil, and turning my birthstone ring backwards to look like a wedding ring when I was a little girl.

Now at fifteen years old, I find myself praying for my future husband and thinking not about the wedding but about the marriage after the ring is on my finger.

Whoever he is, I pray for him, the husband who will love me for who I am. Not only the pretty girl he married at twenty-four, but the mother of his children who will possibly gain a few pounds. I dream of a husband, the father of my children, who will treat me with respect and share a common faith with me. As the wrinkles accumulate on our faces, we will be able to remember the wonderful years we have shared together.

—A. B. L., Washington Township, NJ

I feel that most people believe that boys are completely hormone driven and that we have no self-control when comes to most things. That may be true for some boys, and maybe even for a majority, but some of us do try our best to behave ourselves. We do not all go out and make wrong choices on the weekends. I am tired of being punished by girls for something I didn't do but somebody of the same gender as me did.

—J. B. Lutes, Danville, IL

I hope to find someone who loves me truly, madly, and deeply. I pray I'll find someone who would never think of abusing me or cheating on me. I hope he is reliable, responsible, and patient; someone who gets things done. I want him to remember important occasions and be romantic. I hope he is intelligent, trusting, honest, and trustworthy. I hope he is strong, brave, gentle, and sensitive. I want him to tell me when he has a problem. I want him to be willing to compromise. I hope we'll have similar and different interests and dreams. I hope he has optimism and a good sense of humor. I don't want him to be afraid to cry sometimes. I hope he will know Jesus and is serious about religion. Although I dream that he will be handsome and rich, I would rather he be all of the above instead.

—Rachel Kline, Anniston, AL

127

If there was one idea that I could convey to members of the opposite sex about my gender, I would communicate the message that men want respect just as much as women want respect. Men are stereotypically viewed as unemotional con artists who manipulate the feelings of women in order to elicit sex. However, I believe that men are not rightfully portrayed in this description. Instead I think that most men, just like women, wish to form lasting emotional bonds with a special person. Men may put on a facade to hide their emotions. However, that does not mean they do not want to be respected in loving and committed relationships.

—Bob D., Cincinnati, OH

Don't be shy. Hold us. Make sure you let us know how you feel. If you're scared, **chances are we are too.** . . . You see, we're **not that different** after all. If you promise to understand, we **promise to do the same** for you.

—Melissa Medina, Seattle, WA

He'll wake me up at one in the morning **just to tell me** he loves me because it **couldn't wait** until morning.

—Bridget Nichole, Harper Woods, MI

I want to **share everything** with my future partner— experiences, stories, secrets, jokes, ambitions—which means that my partner and I will have to be **best friends** before we fall in love.

—Mary Kate Behan, West Chester, OH

My hope for my future life partner is that he is as **passionate about Christianity** as I am. I hope we can **raise our children** with the same passion so they will someday have the **power to change** the world.

—Dana Gatto, Drexel Hill, PA

A life partnership means that you **love everything** about your partner—even the things that you hate. It means that your partner's weaknesses are your strengths.

—Wesley P. Lockett, Salt Lake City, UT

What do you wish people of the opposite sex knew about people of your gender?

What is your prayer, wish, hope, or dream for your future life partner?

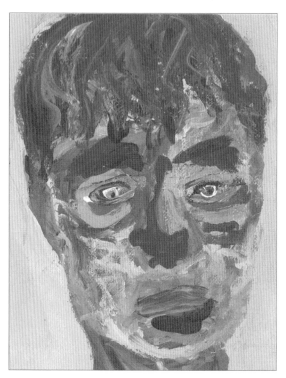

Art by Steven Roe, Winona, MN

I was on the school bus, dwelling on an event that had happened earlier that day. Then my eyes turned toward a girl walking on the sidewalk. She was blind yet didn't seem to have a **care in the world.** Something hit me then and there. I was so **preoccupied with the past** that I was missing out on the picturesque scenery God made.

—Jennifer Price, Altoona PA

Even though I knew that two-year-old boy for only a short hour, I had come to love him. **I love him** because he acted **as the trigger** that enabled me to experience God like few others have been able to.

—Kate Nicholas, Little Rock, AR

ABOUT WHAT IS HOLY

I left the porch and looked up at the sunrise. The colors were so **intense and beautiful.**

—T. J. Meyer, Hermitage, PA

Holy ground to me is a place where I can just relax and do some thinking. It is also a place where I can be at **peace with God and myself.**

—Kevin Butler, Harper Woods, MI

It was a bitterly cold night, and the wind coming off the mountain cut into my sleeping bag, seeming to freeze all my extremities. My makeshift shelter seemed to be made out of tissue the way gusts of air would rattle and disfigure the tarp. I was utterly terrified of falling asleep surrounded by the unfamiliar noises. I was exhausted from keeping myself awake, trying to stay warm, and praying every prayer taught in Catholic schools. As I anticipated morning, I decided to stick my head out to see if the sun was beginning to peek out from behind the mountains. Instead I saw a multitude of stars shining down on me. The cold air changed to a warm breeze, and my fear changed to an immense sensation of inner peace. I fell asleep under the stars, comforted by the beauty and majesty of God's presence with a feeling that has never left me.

I will never forget the summer of 2001, when a few of my schoolmates and I ventured off into the wilderness. Deep in the mountains I discovered a passion for God and his creations that I never knew I had. On my one night of solitude, my spirituality was most transformed by God's awesome presence that cold starry night.

—Heather Ryanne Carrillo, Little Rock, AR

After entering a seemingly boring park, my family and I ventured deep into the woods, where we discovered a wide river decorated with colorful rocks and sparkling white waterfalls. The surrounding forest, thick and lush, reminded me of a tropical rain forest. Having plodded through the thick summer air, we couldn't resist the lure of the cool mountain waters. We plunged in and played in the strong currents, splashing one another like little kids. We saw a towering thirty-foot waterfall upstream. I waded toward it quickly, until I could feel the intense spray of the waterfall stinging my face. I reached my hand out and felt the enormous power of the plummeting water. I stared up in awe for nearly a minute, then looked at the deep green forest, and glanced behind me at the rest of my family, who were eagerly catching up to me to share in the overwhelming experience. At that moment I was completely in touch with God. I breathed a silent prayer, "Thank you Lord."

—Nick Bockey, Delphos, OH

It had been a rough day. I lay motionless on my bed, staring at the scattered textbooks on my floor, and realized that the intensity of my headache matched the pounding of the rain outside. I was disorganized with my paperwork and my emotions. My confusion, indecisiveness, and apprehension were strewn like the papers. I had lost touch with my friends all summer, and the beginning of school had brought nothing but loneliness. A tear ran down my cheek, but the phone interrupted my misery.

"How's school?" asked a familiar voice.

"Nothing special," I mumbled.

"Nothing special? They have you, don't they?"

I put down the phone and broke into hysterics. For the first time, I realized God was the reason this person was in my life. Courage poured through my veins, for I knew I wasn't alone. There could not have been any more sunshine on a gloomier day.

—Laryssa Wirstiuk, Morristown, NJ

In a time of terror, many fear the unknown. Actions brought on by misunderstanding have left millions to strive for the only peace of mind they can find—the Church. Such inspiration led me to questions in my own mind. I recollect a time when grades had no importance to me, and the beginning of our eighth-grade field trip was under way. When we arrived, there were numerous events, but the one I remember leaving with a feeling of unity and oneness with God was on the last night. Our entire class gathered in a circle, and the lights were turned off. A single candle was lit, and we were asked to sit closer to the candle if our relationship with God was close, and vice versa. There we told stories and intimate secrets no one could have guessed. This sharing of stories opened up my mind to God's presence in my everyday life. After the retreat, I felt God more present in my life, and I felt more able to respond to God's calls.

—Carlos Cutting, Dallas, TX

About a year ago, I had an intense experience of the presence of God that I will never forget. Growing up, I was considered an outcast. I never fit in with the "in crowd." I had just finished playing football with my friends when they had to go home. I sat down by myself on the lowest bleacher and was staring down at my sneakers, feeling alone and depressed. Just then, I began to cry. I watched my first tear fall on the ground, and at the same time I watched a raindrop fall next to me. It began to pour. As of that moment, I knew that I would never be alone and that God will always be crying with me to comfort me in my sorrows.

—Kristie Lucking, Rockaway Park, NY

Children are truly one of God's greatest gifts. There is something completely awe inspiring about their mannerisms, their habits, and their simplicity. It is amazing how they laugh and play their games, how they dance and find joy and thrill in every moment of life. But what is especially astounding about children is the way they sing.

I discovered how powerful song can be this past summer while I was volunteering as a counselor at a summer day camp. One morning I was

I believe that one time I was in the presence of the holy. This encounter was about six months ago. It happened in church one day while I was listening to the homily. I was staring at the altar when all the lights and reflections got really bright. This went on for only a few seconds. Then I realized what it was.

I have an idea of what might have triggered it. A few weeks before this experience, my grandmother was diagnosed with cancer. I did not really want to talk about it, but deep down in my heart there was a large amount of sadness. I had to stay strong for my family. When this encounter happened, it took away all the sadness and agony, and I believed in God even more.

—Brandon Sparacino, Watertown, NY

walking toward the auditorium where the campers were assembled and just as I opened the door, a feeling of God's presence burst open inside me. The children were singing to God.

—Diane Pflug, Jamaica Estates, NY

During January of 1999, my Dad was extremely ill in the hospital. I was overwrought with emotions. I needed someone to talk to, someone who would listen to my every word without interrupting, someone I could share my fears with, and someone who could help me. I turned to God. For each night that my father was in the hospital, I prayed the rosary. As I lay in my bed with my eyes tightly shut and the rosary beads braided between my fingers, I felt the presence of God greater than any other time in my life. I felt as if he was in the room, comforting me with his warmth and assurance, praying along with me for the recuperation of my father. Three months later, my dad made a miraculous recovery and was out of the ICU. He is now home and doing well. God has touched my life in a very special way. Because of my experience, I know he is with me every step of the way.

—Susan Traina, Washington Township, NJ

The Eucharist is a great mystery that no one can exactly define, but to me it is the greatest way to actually meet God. Since the beginning of time, humans have searched deeply to find out what God is and how to meet him. Luckily, for me, all I have to do is go to a Catholic church, and they actually present me with God. It's truly amazing when I wait to receive the Eucharist because right in front of me is Jesus Christ, the greatest historical figure ever and the person I owe everything to for giving me the chance to live a better life and an immortal life. People get excited over meeting a human celebrity, but how many get excited over direct union with God? To me, receiving God is much better than meeting any person of fame, and that's the bottom line.

—Scott Adams, Lorain, OH

The Eucharist means so much to me. It is a symbol of God's love for the world. He loved each of us enough to die for us, and that helps me remember how special and important each person is.

The Eucharist is also a place for me to go when I am tired or struggling. No matter what my life has been like lately, I can go to the Eucharist and unload my troubles on Christ. I thank him for his love and forgiveness, and I am very glad for the Eucharist!

—Christine, Scio, OR

It was Tuesday morning, and I was in my first period class. Suddenly the loud speaker came on, followed by a long silence. A strange feeling came over me as if I already knew. Our principal said, "Today at 9:10 a.m., two hijacked planes crashed into the World Trade Centers in New York City." These words put a bigger gap between already distant races but also brought a widespread sense of unity and want for freedom. It would be impossible to get something good out of such a tragedy, but the unity achieved has made me believe more in the

I've always had a strong love for God and the Holy Mass, and a desire to live in his love. However, it has only been since I entered high school that I began to realize the true value of the Eucharist in my life. During the school year, I'm close to a daily communicant, and my faith in the True Presence of the Eucharist has guided me and strengthened me whenever I receive. Devotion to Jesus in the Eucharist has helped me to overcome difficulties, to be strong in times of distress, and to more fully appreciate the many gifts God has given me. Attending daily Mass gives me a chance to take time out to pray and to be uplifted before a hectic day. When I say amen, I am responding that I believe in Christ's true presence in the Eucharist, and I am ready for him to enter into my heart.

—Eric E. Ruszala, Saint Clair Shores, MI

presence of God in me and in everyone. At that moment I felt something changing and growing inside me. It was an indescribable feeling, one that made me happy and sad at the same time. If no higher power exists, then how is all this possible?

—A. L., Troy, NY

"Here I am, the servant of the Lord; let it be with me according to your word" (Luke 1:38). At a young age, Mary spoke these words to express her agreement with God's plan. Because she is such a great hero and role model, I would definitely want to meet her if given the opportunity. Knowing that she could have been stoned to death because she was with child, she still agreed to bear Jesus, showing her strong faith in God. Because of this, she is my model of divine trust in the Father. The Holy Mother stands as an example of courage and fidelity in my life journey with God. Am I willing to let God's plan happen within me as Mary did?

—Jenny Warnecke, Delphos, OH

One evening, my Confirmation class entered into a crowded chapel to pray in front of the Blessed Sacrament. Earlier in the week, I had prayed to the Lord for faith and reassurance of his existence in my life. My teacher told the class that we could pray for as long as we wished. Because the chapel is very small and the class is large, people were kneeling on the floor, and the pews were crammed with students. My friend and I were lucky enough to get a pew, but we were so close that we touched. While I was praying, I felt the presence of my friend because we were so packed together. Just before I opened my eyes, I could still feel him. But when I opened my eyes, I was alone in the pew. I knew that the presence I felt was the Holy Spirit. A couple hours later it hit me: the strong presence I felt was God answering my prayers. God answered my prayer for reassurance and faith by gracing me during prayer.

—Trevor Marxen, Mission Hills, CA

During the time of Jesus, women were looked upon as inferior. However, thanks to the Gospel of Luke and other sources, we have some information about Mary, the mother of Jesus. The Gospels paint a picture of her as courageous, obedient, loyal, and loving. She put her own reputation in jeopardy when she agreed to bear the Son of God. Becoming pregnant before marriage was a terrible scandal that was only made more scandalous by the fact that the husband-to-be was not the father of the baby. Mary raised Jesus only to endure the pain and horrific torture of watching him suffer, knowing all the while that not a thing could be done. Mary would be an interesting person to meet because she is the model of the perfect Catholic. She said yes to God's call and never once doubted that "for God all things are possible" (Matthew 19:26).

—Barbara Gallé, Demarest, NJ

I found out I was hearing-impaired when I was in the sixth grade. When I was told, my spirit was shattered. Later that year I found out about Saint Katherine Drexel's miracles and how she is known for having healed deaf children. After learning what she had done for many others, I would love to meet her. I pray to her daily in hopes that my own hearing

Once again, they are calling me. I stand anxiously, barely moving as I am slowly ascending to my mark. Many others are here, some very different from me, but we are all here for the same reason. I am going to be alive again! I will know what heaven is while on earth! With each step I take, my heart and soul fly closer to the heavens until my body is so lonely that they must return to nourish it. I see others ahead who have received the gift already. I am jealous of them and wish that I could be there, but I must wait. I can think only of the happiness my soul will receive. I cannot wait any longer to be with Jesus. It is finally my turn, and I receive my gift from the priest. It is the gift of the Eucharist.

—Kevin Patrick Stoner, Wilmington, DE

The person from the Bible I would like to meet would have to be Moses. I would like to meet him because he was a great leader, and he got to talk to and see God. I would like to ask him how life was while he was living. I would like to ask him if he really parted the Red Sea, and what it was like seeing it parted. I would also ask him what it was like to wander in the desert for forty years and if he ever get lost. Another question I

will be restored, even though my doctors said I will lose all of my hearing by the age of twenty-one. From praying to Saint Katherine, the most wonderful thing is happening. I went to my doctor, and he said my hearing is improving. I feel like Saint Katherine has given me something I thought I had lost forever. I would love to meet her and thank her for the blessing she bestowed upon me.

—Jayda Pugliese, Philadelphia, PA

As I think about what significance the Eucharist has in my life, receiving it at Mass on Sunday comes to mind. Receiving the Eucharist every Sunday enables me to become closer to God and my religion. After becoming closer to God, I reflect upon what God has given me. God has blessed me with a wonderful, caring family who loves me dearly. God has given me everything I need to lead a happy joyous life. The Eucharist allows me to experience God's presence. After receiving the Eucharist for the first time, I began to understand my religion more clearly. The Eucharist is very significant in my life. It helps me to become closer to God and enables me to better understand my religion.

—Katie Lynn Podlas, Riverhead, NY

would like to ask is what it was like to control all the people in the desert. It must have been hard keeping everyone happy. The last question I would like to ask Moses is how he felt when he didn't get to enter the Promised Land.

—Curtis, Altoona, PA

The Eucharist maintains a powerful presence in my life and the lives of those around me. Without this lifesaving element of spirituality, I as a sinner, could never be cleansed and would not even have a glimmer of hope of someday entering the pearly gates of heaven, striding past Saint Peter and stepping onto the streets of gold. The Eucharist is a constant reminder of the fact that Jesus died on the cross for me and for all so that our sins may be forgiven. Accepting the Eucharist is like being armed with the weapons of the Holy Spirit, and after receiving it I feel prepared to tackle the next leg of my spiritual journey. In every accomplishment that I strive for and in all that I commit myself to, the Eucharist acts as a reminder that it should all be for the greater glory of God.

—M. R. B., Rocky Hill, CT

I would most like to meet Abraham, because he had such unfaltering faith in God that he would do anything that the Lord asked of him. Abraham was willing to lay down the life of his own son, Isaac, because God had commanded him to do so. Abraham longed and prayed for God to send him and his wife, Sarah, a son, and after his wish was granted, he obeyed the wishes of God and prepared to kill his son. This shows his devout faith in God. He always trusted in God no matter what his trouble was; whether it was being the father of Israel, having as many descendants as there are stars in the sky, or in laying down the life of his own son. I admire Abraham so much because I believe we can all take example from the way he lived his life. God will always take care of us no matter what trouble or problem we have in life as long as we trust in him. We should all try to have ceaseless faith in God just as Abraham did.

—Anna Reik, Danville, IL

In my opinion, picking only one person from the entire Bible is a no-brainer. Without a doubt, the one person I would most like to meet is Jesus Christ. Jesus is the center of history and is a universal compassionate savior for all humanity. He understands everybody and is merciful to all. Jesus is forgiving, trustworthy, and an all around people-person.

Hopefully I will one day meet up with Jesus in the Reign of God. I will ask him questions about his life on earth. How did it feel to perform miracles? Were the twelve Apostles a great group of friends? What were your teenage years like?

Meeting a person like Jesus Christ would most likely leave me speechless; however, his awe-inspiring friendliness, humility, and mercy could make me come alive. Meeting my personal savior would truly be overwhelming!

—David Hayson, Delphos, OH

Aside from Jesus, the person from biblical time I would most like to meet would be Leah, the first wife of Jacob. This is for many reasons. Leah was not very attractive, but because she was the older daughter, it was customary she be married first. Jacob fell in love with Rachel, Leah's beautiful younger sister. Jacob was deceived when he married Leah. He believed it was Rachel, and Leah was aware that he was a husband to her only out of obligation. Leah bore three sons and named them for the surrounding circumstances in her life. She gave birth to Reuben ("the Lord has seen that I am not loved"), Simeon ("the Lord has heard my pain"), and Levi ("now my husband will attach himself to me"). However, after giving birth to her fourth son, Leah named him Judah, which translates to "I will praise the Lord." Leah stopped looking at the world around her and decided that she was in control of her own destiny. It was Leah who bore the twelve tribes of Israel, and, at her death, she was buried with her husband, Jacob. I would love to meet her and thank her for the profound life she led. I am impressed with the way she thanked God for all that had been given to her, even after all the negative experiences in her life.

—Elyse N. Maloni, Buffalo, NY

If I could meet anyone from the Bible, I would choose Peter. I would choose Peter because he had a close and personal relationship with Jesus. I would like to hear all of Peter's stories about Jesus. I would like to hear from someone who knew Jesus personally because sometimes I find it difficult to believe in Jesus based solely on faith. But if I could speak to someone who knew Jesus and hear that person proclaim his Word, then my faith in Christ would grow tremendously.

I would also like to ask Peter about his martyrdom. I would like to speak to someone who had convictions so strong that he was willing to give up his own life. I believe that if he was so strongly committed to Christ, he would be able to offer me something that would dramatically enhance my faith in God and Jesus Christ.

—Rob Haverkamp, Cincinnati, OH

If I could meet any person from the Bible, I would want to meet Peter. I think I would relate well with him. We all know he wasn't perfect. He didn't always understand what Jesus meant. He even denied Jesus three times when Jesus needed him the most. I know I'm not perfect either. I also don't understand everything Jesus teaches and have even denied Jesus. So Peter and I have some things in common. Yet Jesus always forgave Peter and even chose him as the leader of the people Jesus would leave behind on earth. There must be something special about Peter if Jesus chose him to be the rock on which he would build his Church, and I would be honored with the chance to find out what Peter's special something is.

—Christy Abbott, Perryville, MO

For me, each new day reminds me of the Savior's presence in my life. The question is whether or not I have opened my heart and mind to let our heavenly King show me his love and splendid wonders.

—Alexandra Chapman, Saint Joseph, MI

It happened during Eucharistic Adoration. I was praising and worshipping Jesus, asking for the Holy Spirit to help me not keep him in a box and not to anticipate, to just let something happen. And it did. It was strange. I felt that I was seeing what happened to Jesus on his final day. His scourging, his crown of thorns, his torturous march up Golgotha, and his Crucifixion. He let me know that he endured such harsh treatment out of love for us. Throughout the experience I felt grief, and I asked why he had to do this, because it was not fair. I also asked him if I could help relieve some of his suffering, but he wouldn't let me.

—Joseph, Altoona, PA

I feel the presence of God every day of my life. Before I go to sleep, when I pray for God's protection, I feel God's arms around me. When I feel that my life is as bad as it can get and that the struggle is not worth it, I feel God's grace and peace flowing through me, reminding me of how blessed I am.

I see God every day in the faces of my little cousins, in my sisters, in my parents, and in my grandmother. I feel God in their embrace.

I can discern God's fingerprint in the bark of a tree. I discover how his footprints form lakes. God's presence is everywhere. God is with me all day, every day.

—Emilee, Vicksburg, MS

The night of September 11, 2002, I was very frightened because I did not know what was going to become of the terrorist attacks. I sat in my room, closed my eyes, and cried. Then, as I prayed I felt a calmness come over me. I trusted in God that no matter what the outcome that day, my family and I would be safe.

—Jessica, Philadelphia, PA

If I had a chance to meet anyone from the Bible, I would choose John the Baptist. I would choose him because he is the man who baptized Jesus. He told the world to stop looking at themselves and John the Baptist and to start looking to Jesus, for he is the Savior. John didn't ask to share the spotlight with Jesus. He stepped aside and went into the shadows so that everyone would focus on Jesus, not Jesus and John the Baptist. He sacrificed his fame for the greater good of the world. You would be hard pressed to find a person more in touch with God and God's plan than John the Baptist.

—Paul Namey, Hermitage, PA

Have you ever had an intense experience of the presence of God, a sense of being in the presence of the holy? Can you describe that experience and name what may have triggered it?

What saint or person from the Bible would you most like to meet? Why?

What is the significance of the Eucharist in your life?

Sticking to the gender perspective genre

of *She Said . . . He Said . . .* , we invited two people who
have worked in gender-specific settings to read and review the
responses we received and to offer their observations and
reflections about what they think young people feel and think
about life and faith.

Janet Claussen is one of the founding mothers of the Voices
Project and started an all-girl religion class in her coeducational
Catholic high school in Atlanta, Georgia. She is the author of
Awakening: Challenging the Culture with Girls and *Biblical Women:
Exploring Their Stories with Girls* and the co-editor of *Listen for a
Whisper: Prayers, Poems, and Reflections by Girls,* all published by
Saint Mary's Press. Janet is a former parish youth minister and
has worked with groups of women and girls throughout the
country.

K. Sean Buvala is the national director of the Center for
Creative Ministry *(www.creativeministry.com),* based in Phoenix,
Arizona. He is also the director of youth ministry for Saint
Bernadette Parish in Scottsdale, Arizona, where he ministers
with youth in small gender-based church communities. He is
especially proud of his long-term boys' group, affectionately
calling the boys his "lab rats."

Both Janet and Sean are parents of four children each, and
they believe strongly that opportunities for life and faith sharing
in gendered groups can lead young people to greater under-
standings of self, each other, and God.

In addition to sharing their observations, Janet and Sean
offer some ideas for using the book with gender-specific
groups. Both Janet and Sean offer their insights at various
conferences and workshops throughout the country.

As I poured over the nearly seven hundred entries from young people across the country, I was initially amazed at how few gender differences there appeared to be on the surface. I was intentionally looking for differences, hoping they would shout at me and provide further confirmation that the worlds of adolescent girls and boys are distinct. Instead, I was amazed that the reflections of these young people often defied my gender stereotypes. However, subsequent readings and a closer look with my gender lens revealed subtle but crucial differences in the perspectives of the writers.

The most obvious difference was the ratio of girls' responses to boys' responses. Girls submitted almost 75 percent of the total. Not surprising, considering that girls are considered more verbal than boys—even from infancy! The teacher in me knows that the adolescent girls I taught were less likely to ask how long a writing assignment had to be. They seemed to be more at home in the genre of sharing thoughts and feelings in journals and reflections. The boys I taught liked the world of ideas and oral debate—the more controversial the topic, the more involved they became. In mixed-gender groups, the girls often deferred to the boys in these heated discussions. They seemed reluctant to express disagreement. They were more concerned about being nice.

Of those who submitted responses, not only did the girls write more than the boys, but they favored certain topics. Most of the topics remained fairly proportionate to the three-to-one ratio of girls to boys. However, on the topic of friendship, girls' entries outnumbered boys' five to one, confirming my sense of the importance of relationships in girls' lives. Research as academic as Carol Gilligan's *In a Different Voice* or as popular as John Gray's *Men Are from Mars and Women Are from Venus*, has further highlighted these gender variations. As a woman, former girl adolescent, and mother to a young-adult daughter, I feel that the experts affirm my own experience of this age-old phenomenon.

Although their responses were similar, the girls' language about friendship was slightly different from that of their male counterpart's. While trust was a recurring theme, the boys spoke more frequently about loyalty, truth, and honesty, while the girls focused on empathy, understanding, and caring. The boys wanted to make the distinction between acquaintance and friend, while the girls tended to mention the idea of a best friend. Living in and looking at the world of females, I think girls collect friends like trophies, and the word *best* is a matter of degree. Relationships can be a girl's agony and her ecstasy. When they are going well, all is right in the world. Conversely, relationships gone sour can result in heartache.

Another popular topic among both the boys and girls was the greatest value they learned from their parents. Over-whelmingly positive about the topic, our writers often focused on how appreciative they were of their parents' good example and unconditional love. The values of listen-ing and communicating in parent-teen relationships was at the top of the list.

The fears of the girls and boys seemed more gender specific than their thoughts about parental values. The response that was most frequent for both boys and girls was the fear of failure, which they mentioned far more than death. Failure is defined by how well the writers will do in college and in their careers. Girls were more likely than boys to say that they feared being alone—another sign of how important relationships are for girls. When asked about the storm that Jesus could calm in their lives, both the boys and girls spoke of loss and stress affecting them in similar ways.

Both the boys and girls found happiness in spending time with other people. The girls focused on ways of being, while the boys focused on things they liked doing, especially sports. The girls mentioned the joys of volunteer work, family and friends, simple acts of kindness, and times of prayer and solitude. When asked about experiences of the presence of God, the girls were more likely to name encounters with people, especially in tragic moments, while the boys found God more often in creation and isolation. However, both mentioned retreat moments and religious settings as power-ful times to encounter the Divine. By nature, girls in general seem to be more comfortable in communal settings—both religious and secular—and their writings reflect this tendency.

Injustices, temptations, tough Church teachings, and questions for Jesus were topics that revealed the moral concerns of the boys and girls. Their desire to please others helped them overcome personal temptations—fairly typical of the moral development of adolescents. A few girls mentioned their struggle with sexual temptations, and one boy asked Jesus for a frank but honest "clarification about temptations of the flesh." I could almost hear this young man in a one-on-one conversation asking, "God, what were you thinking?!"

The topics evil, suffering, and injustice in the world gave me deep insight into the minds of young people. The controversial issues abortion, racism, capital punishment, war, and violence came up the most. The girls were more specific about their concerns and questions, while the boys stayed in the "meaning of life" mode. My experience teaching peace and justice tells me that girls are often more receptive to countercultural ideas, especially nonviolent ways of solving conflict. Several of our female writers mentioned the futility of meeting violence with violence in reference to the terrorist attacks of September 11, 2001. However, one eloquent young male wrote about love and compassion healing the wounds of war, bullying, and hateful crimes. This is evidence that certain values that we often stereotypically name feminine or masculine can be found in either males or females.

The questions that I thought would generate the most disparity were specifically about gender differences, but I was a bit surprised by the responses. The boys who chose to write on these topics—what they wanted in a life partner and what they wanted girls to know about their own gender—expressed sentiments very similar to the girls'. The boys wanted girls to know that they were more than willing to share their feelings and that they could be sensitive. And girls wanted to defy stereotypes as well, although they were anxious to offer bits of advice for boys, like "Don't break up with me in an instant message on the computer!"

In terms of what they would look for in a life partner, almost all the girls and boys wanted to find a soul mate with whom they could share themselves fully. I wanted to do a bit of matchmaking with these young people, but only six boys answered this question compared to twenty-two girls, so my "dating game" would have been a bit uneven. Two girls brought up Prince Charming by name, but an equal number said that Jesus was the role model for their life partner. Smart girls.

While Prince Charming is a romantic ideal that lives only in fairy tales (and we never get to see what "happily ever after" really means), Jesus is a model for members of both genders who seek to live our their humanity in relationship with others. As he lived out his human existence on this earth, Jesus exhibited characteristics that we associate with both men and women. He was strong and loyal, yet vulnerable and open. Jesus wept, and he got angry. He intuitively knew when someone in the crowd touched the hem of his cloak and yet could amaze the elders in the synagogues with his intellect. Jesus' interactions with both men and women remind us that what we name as masculine and feminine goes beyond our physical gender. As people made in the image of God, we are called to mutual respect and healthy communication, the keys to healthier relationships. And I believe that relationships are essential to being the kind of people God created us to be.

Janet Claussen

Janet Claussen

One of the frequent observations that both Janet and I had in reading the submissions for this book was the disparity between the number of girls who answered the questions and the number of boys who answered questions. This reminded me of the many boys I know. I call them the "long thinkers."

Long thinkers can and will answer questions; it just takes them longer to put their answers into words. I have several of these long thinkers in my parish gender-based groups. For instance, just about every time I ask Steven a question, he will slowly rub his forehead as if he is wiping mental perspiration from the brow of his brain while he retorts, "I just don't think very often about the questions you ask." Jacob will join in the conversations of faith and feelings, essence and spirit only "after you guys start talking for a while so that my mind can get the words for what I am thinking."

In these pages, you can hear the long thinkers trying to make sense of the questions. They sometimes answer in stilted, formal sentences, almost as if asking, "Is this what I am supposed to be writing?" One of the boys in this book penned: "We have too much going through our minds at once, and we get frustrated mentally and lose track of our thoughts. . . . Either we are not completely sure what to think, or we feel forced to say something and then get scared" (page 128).

I had quite a few thoughts about boys as I was reading through and reflecting on the responses from the boys in this book. Boys are active, and many function best when they are moving. Several of the boys' answers to "What makes you happy?" were directly related to movement and sports, such as cycling, snowboarding, and basketball. Sports and other physical activities help boys reset and clear their minds and hearts.

I noticed how often both genders mentioned fear of failure. I was caught by how often boys feared failing as a father and husband, as if being a parent and a spouse is simply a result of doing things right rather than being authentic. You might be as surprised and challenged as I was by one young man's fear that being a handicapped father would be an embarrassment to his children. Parents, teachers, counselors, and youth ministers must help adolescent males learn that *who* they are is more important that *what* they are.

I also noticed how the boys frequently mentioned their need for, as one contributor put it, "the few distinguished and amazing people" that make up the small circle of a boy's friends. In these reflections from boys, friendships are most often described in terms of loyalty, trust, and the willingness to "drop anything" and be present with and for one another. Hunger for emotional intimacy knows no gender, and many of the boys who sent in responses expressed their need for it.

Boys are capable of wonder, awe, and deep spirituality. These recognitions often come from external sources first, such as nature or events, and then internalize them. Do we sometimes assume that boys are not as spiritual as girls? Many of the writings in this book tell us otherwise.

Because many boys have a limited emotional vocabulary, writing seems an appropriate medium through which they can gather the right expressions without being rushed. For the long thinkers, writing activities can be exceptionally rewarding. Writing allows them a chance to work as slowly and deliberately as they may need, picking and choosing from the flotsam of thoughts often contained in their minds. With boys, knowledge is power and security, so allow the boys in this book to be the mentors for the boys you know.

K. Sean Buvala

The selections included in *She Said . . . He Said . . .* come from a diverse group of high-school-aged young people from across the country. In some cases we have published reflections in their entirety, and in other instances we have chosen just a few lines or a particularly insightful quote. In this book you will find the thoughts of girls side-by-side with those of boys to create a conversational format with the intention of illustrating gender perspective. *She Said . . . He Said . . .* is a great tool for communication, specifically concerning gender. It shows how we can all get to the same place working from different starting places or perspectives. Young people will want to use this book on their own as they recognize familiar feelings and thoughts. Questions and space for their own reflections offer an opportunity to join the conversation and can lead to further reflection for individuals, family members, or groups.

This book would be a helpful gift to parents and to adults who work with teens in either a spiritual or secular setting. The writings offer insightful wit and impressive wisdom on the life and faith of young people. Each chapter, or the book in its entirety, makes an excellent discussion starter for mixed-gender or gender-specific meetings. If you gather with all girls, you might use the boys' writings to delve into an understanding of why they think as they do and vice versa. The book may also be used in the following ways:

- to start discussion on topics important to teens
- to incorporate reflections into a classroom session or a parish ministry program that focuses on gender differences
- to create a "name that gender" game using the quotations and reflections
- to encourage journaling opportunities and writing exercises using the questions provided at the end of each chapter
- to compare the writings in *She Said . . . He Said . . .* with the young people's own experience

- to open intergenerational or family conversation starters
- to incorporate quotations or parts of reflections into prayer services
- to train adults by asking them to compare their answers to the questions in the back of each chapter to the reflections in the chapter

Finally, regardless of gender, we invite you—teachers, parents, youth workers, and teens—to reflect on your own responses to the questions in this book. The uses of *She Said . . . He Said . . .* are limited only by one's creativity. If you find a unique way to use this book, we would love to hear about it. Write to the editor, Laurie Delgatto, at Saint Mary's Press, 702 Terrace Heights, Winona, MN 55987-1318, e-mail her at *ldelgatto@smp.org,* or visit us on the Web at *www.smp.org.*

INDEX

INDEX

INDEX

INDEX

INDEX